Now Is The Time To Walk In The Spirit

By Lori Granniss

I dedicate this book to my wonderful husband David and my amazing children Landon and Logan. I love you and pray for you as you walk in the Spirit. Each day is a new and exciting adventure with you.

I also dedicate this book to Natalie and Kevin Messerschmidt. Besides the Lord, there's no one who loved me more during my wilderness season. You prayed for me endless times. I thank you for never giving up on me. Thank you for answering endless questions for this book.

CONTENTS

1. Now is the Time   9
2. Hearing God's Voice   13
3. Praying In The Spirit   19
4. Overcoming the Wilderness 31
5. Identity In Christ   39
6. Walking In Purity   43
7. Worship   49
8. Following God's Lead   55
9. Humility   63
10. Prophetic Prayer   69
11. Loving The Unlovely   77
12. Share Your Testimony   83
13. God's Power is Made
    Perfect In Our Weakness   87
14. Rest and Restoration   91
15. Overcoming Fear   99
16. Uniting In Love   105
17. Praying in Faith   111
18. Revival   115

Introduction:

For the past few years, there has been a huge desire in my heart to write a book. I know that God placed this desire there because I am not a natural English writer. I write math curriculum. I am a math person. I love numbers. I celebrated in college when I finished my last English class, and that was mainly because I was finished writing long papers. However, when God writes through me, the words are very powerful, and I realize that it's all Him. God's strength is made perfect in my weakness. This book contains downloads that God spoke to me to help you. God says this book is to "accelerate the church," meaning things that would normally take someone years to learn can be learned quickly. If you are reading this right now, you are revealing that you are hungry for more of God. This book can show you how to live the Christian life God intended for you. You are His dearly beloved and chosen one. I pray that God will give you eyes to see and ears to hear what He has to say to your heart.

This book may shake you up, challenge denominational beliefs, and make your heart want to go against the flow of cautious Christianity. Beth Moore held a simulcast on the topic of being audacious. We need to be audacious! After you read this book, you may need an audacious boldness to agree with God, even if some of your Christian friends won't step out and believe everything the Bible says. I've written about subjects that may be hard for you to accept, but God has asked me to write about them. You may not be open to all that I have written, but I promise it is in God's Word. If you are not comfortable with something that you read, that is okay. I always say to please "put topics on a shelf," if you need to, until you have time to ask God questions about them and search them out in the Bible for yourself. This book will teach you how to walk with freedom in the Spirit. In the times we are living in, we need to know how to walk with freedom in the Spirit. I believe that God is starting a great revival. He has revealed this through many intercessors. God gave us a prophetic word for this revival and said that prophetic prayer and humility are keys to discover our roles in this revival. That means that if you don't know how to pray prophetically, you may miss out on this major move of God. This book can equip you with all the tools you need to walk with freedom in the Spirit and be a part of this revival. There has never been a time on Earth where we need to walk with freedom in the Spirit more than we do right now. I pray that as you read this book you will know the truth, and the truth will set you free!

Chapter 1

Now Is The Time!

For he says, "In the time of my favor I heard you, and in the day of salvation I helped you." I tell you, now is the time of God's favor, now is the day of salvation.
2 Corinthians 6:2

I went through a hard wilderness season when I lived in Connecticut. During that time, I had a supernatural experience with God. First, God showed me many examples of how He sent angels to give people messages in the Bible. Then one morning my husband's watch alarm went off at 5 am, although he did not set it. I awoke to an angel in my room who said, "Now is the Time!" I then began singing to myself, "Now, now is the time to worship!" The next two mornings the angel appeared at the same time (5 am), but I was so frightened by the angel that the angel didn't say anything. I wish I had not panicked, but it was very new for me and it was overwhelming. (The next time an angel comes into your room, let me know if you don't panic a little). I began a journey with God to see what the message "Now is the Time" meant. What I didn't know at the time was that God was preparing a way for this book.

As I searched for what the message "Now is the Time" meant, I ran across a teaching from a well-known Connecticut evangelist named Bob Hazlett. He said, "Now is the time, means now is the time in heaven." God created time on Earth for us, and time as it is in heaven is not the same as time on Earth. God showed me that the time in heaven is always now, so I need to have a heavenly mindset. That means that I need to do everything that I can do in my own power to take steps towards my destiny now. The meaning really impacted me.

A while ago, we lived in a tiny house for a few years. We looked for other houses for a while but got to a point where we did not find anything, and we stopped looking. A few months later, God did a miracle and suddenly moved us from our tiny house to a large house. A ministry near us was moving and needed to sell their intern house. It had five bedrooms, five bathrooms, and a pool. Our friend, who is a Realtor, said she could not stop thinking of us so she called us to come see it. We put in an offer that we could afford, and they countered very close to our offer. We accepted, and we felt very shocked and blessed. Normally we would not be able to afford this size house, but with the work it needed and the need the ministry had to get rid of it, God did a miracle in the price.

At a prayer meeting the Lord told us that He was giving me this house for my ministry. My first ministry is my family. I love them with all my heart. I've been blessed to work from home and to be a stay at home mom for twelve years. I also felt God leading us to have a place where missionaries could come and rest and get prayer and deliverance. I prayed that night that God would guide me forward to have missionaries over if that's something that He wanted. My husband was out of town, and I texted a few of my friends to come over and hang out. A friend wrote me back and said that she could stop by my house. She just happened to be a missionary, and I did not realize it. When she was on her way over the Lord said, "Here is your first missionary." My missionary friend was shocked that I had her over for dinner and that I wanted her to tell me her missionary stories. She said she was never really treated special and invited over to dinner for being a missionary before. The next night another friend sent me a reply text to come over, and she happened to be a missionary as well. Within two nights, we had already begun to host missionaries by having them over for dinner. It was a great start to what God had planned for our home.

What promises has God given you? Has He confirmed any dreams in your heart? If so, think about what steps you can take to get closer to your goal. If you have a promise God has given you, try to make a list of the steps that will move you towards your goal. Can you take a class? Or maybe teach a class? Can you volunteer to help kids or the homeless? What area has God called you to? If you don't know, I am going to help you find out what your calling is in the next chapter. Now is the time!

Chapter 2

Now Is The Time to Hear God's Voice

"My sheep hear My voice, and I know them, and they follow Me." John 10:27 (NKJV)

     I love hearing God's voice. It is one of my favorite things in the entire world. God says, "My sheep hear my voice" (John 10:27). This means if we are God's sheep, we hear His voice, whether we recognize it or not. God says, "faith comes by hearing and hearing by the Word of God" (Romans 10:17 NKJV). If we want to hear God's voice often, first we have to believe that He still speaks to us. When we set apart time with Him to read His Word and talk with Him throughout the day, He begins to speak to us. The Holy Spirit lives inside us and He is available to communicate with us anytime, any day. He never sleeps nor slumbers. The verse, faith comes by hearing, reveals to us that we can hear God. We can learn to hear Him in our own unique way.

     God speaks to me the most by giving me pictures in my imagination. He also gives me thoughts that sounds similar to my own thoughts; however, through practice, I have learned when it is God's voice speaking to me. Have you ever said, "God speaks to other people, but He never speaks to me?" I am sure that you have heard the Holy Spirit before. Have you ever thought, "Maybe I should check to see if the oven is still on before I leave the house?" And when you went to check it, you saw that the oven was on? That was the Holy Spirit speaking to you. Some people are very aware of this, and they do a good job of listening to their gut or their instincts. In reality, they are actually very good at listening to the Holy Spirit.

Have you ever written an email and then heard a voice say, "Should I really send this?" Then your browser has an error and crashes. At that time, you may realize, "This is a horrible idea, maybe I shouldn't send this." God may be trying to help you by literally closing your screen. You can retype the email or you can listen to your gut feeling. This gut feeling is often the Holy Spirit speaking to you. You might be really good at listening to God's voice. If not, you can become more aware of when God speaks to you by practicing listening for Him.

Another way you can hear God speak to you is by remembering your dreams. The first time God spoke to me through a dream, He had me study dreams in the Bible. I studied Daniel and Joseph. I also looked at how God spoke to Joseph when the Holy Spirit conceived in Mary. It was going to take something supernatural to get his attention that this was God's plan. Sometimes

God needs to speak to us through a supernatural way to get our attention. Everyone dreams at night, but not everyone remembers their dreams.

I have been a dreamer and have remembered most of my dreams since I was a young girl. When God gave me one of my first significant dreams, we were moving from Texas to Connecticut and we needed to sell two houses, our primary house and our rental house. The rental house had been on the market for about five months, and we were about to put our primary house up for sale. We went to pray over our rental house and began talking with our Realtor about listing our primary house. Soon after this, I had a dream that the first person who came to look at our house would make a full offer. My dream even revealed what we should list as the selling price, which was higher than what the Realtor thought we should ask. We listed our house for sale at a higher price, and every morning I woke up and said, "The first person who looks at our house is going to buy it." Two weeks went by and no one looked at our house, but I had great faith that this was going to happen. Exactly three weeks after we listed it, on a Sunday morning, we got a call that someone wanted to see our house. I cleaned a little extra, and we headed off to church. For the first time, my faith wavered. I had thoughts in my head that said it wasn't going to happen. "I am not sure if they are going to like our house," I said. My husband said, "You have been saying for three weeks that the first person who looks at our house is going to buy it, and believe me, they are." Thankfully he had great faith at that moment. We were told that the people wanted to look at the house again, a great sign! We waited, but they did not call back for a few days. Then we got a call that they did not want to look at the house again because they had just put in an offer. The offer was very close to what we were asking. We countered, and they agreed. Then we got a call that there was an offer on our rental house. God sold both our houses in record time during a season when houses were not selling very well. We were so thankful and we began a journey where we realized that God does speaks through dreams.

We are all called to love people. We also have specific callings on our lives. Do you know your destiny? Do you know what you where designed for? You can ask God what your calling is. He may give you a calling dream. I have had calling dreams. You might dream God uses you to save someone. This might mean you have a call to evangelism. You can also look at where the enemy has attacked you the most to find your purpose or calling. Have you been sick a lot? If so, you are probably called to pray for healing. Was anyone in your family sick often? This usually goes down your family line. Have you struggled with depression? Have you been attacked with mental warfare? You may be called to pray for deliverance. God can use you to help set people free. What area has the enemy attacked you?

God may speak to you through nature. Nature is a place where we can go and spend time with God without distraction. It is also the beauty that God has made. These two things together can really heighten our senses to God. Is there a place in or near your home that you like to spend time with God?

Does God speak to you? What are some things He has said to you recently? What are some ways that He speaks to you? Journaling is a good way to keep track of what the Lord has spoken to you. Journal a few things God is saying to you. I pray that God will speak to your heart today.

_____

_____

_____

_____

_____

_____

_____

_____

_____

_____

_____

_____

_____

_____

_____

_____

Chapter 3

Now Is The Time to Pray in the Spirit

"And pray in the Spirit on all occasions with all kinds of prayers and requests. With this in mind, be alert and always keep on praying for all the Lord's people."
Ephesians 6:18

To pray in the Spirit, we have to be filled with the Spirit. When we accept Christ into our lives we get God's promise of the Holy Spirit. However, we are commanded to be filled with the Holy Spirit (Ephesians 5:18). This filling doesn't just happen automatically. We have to ask for it.

We are told in the Word to put on the armor of God. This is a strategic strategy. The Lord whispered the two words "under armour" to me. I knew He wanted me to seek Him out to see what this meant, so I did. I found that under armour was the Holy Spirit. We've got to pray in the Spirit daily and make sure we put our under armour on so that we can wear the armor of God on top of it. The Holy Spirit lives inside us and with us. With the under armour on, the top armor stays in place. How do we pray in the Spirit in our daily lives? I will reveal what the Lord has shown me about this secret prayer weapon.

When I was 29 years old, I had a dream that I was at a Bible study and someone spoke in tongues. Then someone else interpreted it. When I woke up I decided to spend a while looking into what this dream meant. I was raised in the Baptist denomination, and I love my strong Baptist roots. I was saved and later water baptized at age 7. However, I was not taught anything about tongues in my church. I knew that tongues were in the Bible, so I began to search the Word and I saw that tongues were very encouraged. Paul said, "I wish you could all speak in tongues" (1 Corinthians 14:5a). I prayed that God would do with me whatever He wanted to do as far as tongues were concerned, and I told Him that I was open to whatever He had for me. This is a good prayer to pray. I went through a few months of confession where God brought things to my mind that He wanted me to change in my life. A few months later, I went to a Baptist ladies retreat and knelt down by the lake to pray. Suddenly, I knew that I was about to pray in tongues. Since I was sitting by the pastor's wife and it was a Baptist church, I decided not to pray in tongues out loud. In consideration of those around me, I prayed in tongues only to myself, in my mind. I felt God's love fill me. Heat went from the top of my head to the bottom of my feet.

It was the first time in my life that I felt God's "liquid love" fill me. I experienced what is known as being filled with the Holy Spirit.

This experience I had with the filling of the Holy Spirit led me to an in-depth search of the Scriptures. I decided that I wanted to know everything that was written in the Word, including anything else I should know that I was not taught in church. I learned so much about being filled with the Holy Spirit in Scripture.

What if God meant for Christians to be filled with the Holy Spirit just like the disciples were in the book of Acts? When I searched the scriptures, I found that the Lord does want us to be filled with the Holy Spirit just like the disciples were. He wants to equip us with His power from on high. He never intended for us to walk in our own power. He wants us to yield to Him and walk in the Holy Spirit's power.

Have you ever walked into a church and you felt the Lord's presence? Do you get goosebumps or cry when you feel the Lord's presence? I am a crier when I discern that something is from the Lord. When you walk into a church where the members are filled with the Holy Spirit, you can almost always feel the presence of God. Why is this? The members are filled with the Spirit. They are filled with God's power, and it powerfully affects other people.

Does being filled with the Holy Spirit include speaking in tongues? Yes, it can include speaking in tongues. Speaking in tongues is something that has been done since Pentecost. I did some digging into church history, and I found that in the 1800s there was a Christian theologian named BB Warfield who decided that tongues were not for today. I believe the enemy has used this conclusion to cause great division and pull revelation and power out of the church. If theologians such as BB Warfield mistakenly allowed the enemy to take tongues out of part of the Church, then I want the Lord to put them back. I pray that the Lord would give you eyes to see and ears to hear what He has to say to you about the Holy Spirit.

Did God intend for Christians to be filled with the Holy Spirit around the same time that we have a water baptism? I believe that He intended for the two events to occur close together, and I will show you examples of why I believe this. In Mozambique, missionary Heidi Baker tells stories of children who have had hands laid on them and prayed to be filled with the Holy Spirit before they get water baptized. Many of these children are lifted out of their water baptism, and they immediately begin joyfully speaking in tongues. In America, we tend to make these two events separate, and I think that is okay, but I believe that we must realize that both events are needed to have the fullness of the Holy Spirit's revelation and power for our lives (1 Corinthians 2:10).

Here is an example where salvation and being filled with the Holy Spirit happened to some men who were disciples at the same time. Paul led disciples to salvation and they were filled with the Holy Spirit. They began speaking in tongues and prophesied.

While Apollos was at Corinth, Paul took the road through the interior and arrived at Ephesus. There he found some disciples and asked them, "Did you receive the Holy Spirit when you believed?" They answered, "No, we have not even heard that there is a Holy Spirit." So Paul asked, "Then what baptism did you receive?" "John's baptism," they replied. Paul said, "John's baptism was a baptism of repentance. He told the people to believe in the one coming after him, that is, in Jesus." On hearing this, they were baptized in the name of the Lord Jesus. When Paul placed his hands on them, the Holy Spirit came on them, and they spoke in tongues and prophesied. There were about twelve men in all. Acts 19:1-7

One reason it is good to experience the two events together is that the baptism of the Holy Spirit is sometimes idolized. The enemy can use this event to give believers pride because they see that they have the Holy Spirit's power and that other believers do not. The enemy can sneak a lie of pride to someone, first as a thought. If it is not cast down, it then goes into their heart. If the lie is realized at any point, it can be easily confessed and replaced with the truth. If we look at the filling of the Holy Spirit as an acceleration to do the Lord's work, instead of a monumental turning point in our lives, we can overcome pride.

Look what happens right after the water baptism of Jesus. Just as Jesus was coming out of the water,

He saw heaven being torn open and the Spirit descending on Him like a dove. And a voice came from heaven, "You are my Son, whom I love; with you I am well pleased" (Mark 1:10-12). Jesus had a water baptism and then immediately had an experience with the Holy Spirit. Jesus began His miracles after this experience with the Holy Spirit. The Lord began doing miracles in my life after I was baptized with the Holy Spirit as well. I will tell you more about them later in this book.

Some people call being filled with the Holy Spirit a baptism of the Holy Spirit. It does call this a baptism in the Bible, so I believe it is okay to call it this. In Acts 10, Cornelius has an amazing encounter with an angel who tells him to send men to get Peter. When Peter came, the Bible says that Cornelius was baptized with the Holy Spirit first. Then he was water baptized. I believe he was baptized with the Holy Spirit first to prove that God was opening up salvation to the Gentiles. I love this because it just goes to show that you can't put God in a box, and it really does not matter what order that you are baptized in. Cornelius experienced the Holy Spirit before he was water baptized.

Another example in the Bible is in Acts 8.

"When the apostles in Jerusalem heard that Samaria had accepted the word of God, they sent Peter and John to Samaria. When they arrived, they prayed for the new believers there that they might receive the Holy Spirit, because the Holy Spirit had not yet come on any of them; they had simply been baptized in the name of the Lord Jesus. Then Peter and John placed their hands on them, and they received the Holy Spirit." Acts 8:14-17

The people of Samaria had been water baptized but they had not been baptized with the Holy Spirit. Peter and John laid hands on them and prayed that they might receive the Holy Spirit. Have you ever prayed to be filled with the Holy Spirit? If God knew that it was good for the disciples, then it is also good for you. Paul says, "Do not forbid speaking in tongues" (1 Corinthians 14:39b).

Another way the Bible refers to praying in tongues or in a prayer language is to pray in the Spirit. One of the best parts about praying in the Spirit is that if we don't know what to pray for someone, we can pray in our prayer language or tongues. Right after I was filled with the Holy Spirit, I received a spiritual gift of discernment. My gift would show me when someone needed prayer. I would go to the grocery store and see people that the Lord pointed out needed prayer. The Lord would not usually tell me why they needed prayer. Praying for them in my prayer language silently to myself was powerful because the Holy Spirit knew what they needed. I also usually prayed for salvation and healing for them.

Sometimes when I pray in tongues, later during the day, I suddenly cry and I pray for something for our nation or our world. The Lord told me that my spirit was interpreting my tongue, and I was praying perfectly in God's will. If you cry often, you may have this gift. This is a compassion gift in line with God's heart. This can be scary if this happens to you and you do not realize what is going on. You may wonder why you cry to God randomly, but you are actually interpreting your own tongue. You may also release things as you pray for others. You may feel what they feel and can release a burden that they may not be able to bear. As God pours out His Spirit on His people, this may happen to you often. This is good to be aware of so you don't feel like you are over emotional, when you are actually a mighty intercessor for the Lord.

When you are filled with the Holy Spirit, you get the power of the Holy Spirit. When I was writing this chapter, the Lord woke me up one morning and said, "Tongues are for power." I felt like He was encouraging me and clarifying that He wanted me to write this chapter. When I pray in tongues, I am building myself up in Christ (1 Corinthians 14:4). I am yielding to Him so that He can give me His power. Acts 1:8 says, "But you will receive power when the Holy Spirit has come upon you, and you will be my witnesses in Jerusalem and in all Judea and Samaria, and to the end of the earth." I have heard of many revivals starting after Christians yield to the filling of the Holy Spirit. The Azusa Street Revival began this way. William Seymour waited patiently for the Holy Spirit, and when the Holy Spirit came, a revival started.

Power from the Holy Spirit is not intended for the benefit of man. It is intended to further the Kingdom of Heaven. We need to hear God's revelation to know what to do, and then have God's power to be able to do it. We need to be filled with the Holy Spirit to walk in the Spirit.

God speaks to me mostly through images in my mind, and then I ask Him what they mean. I was in a prayer meeting, and God gave me a strange image in my imagination. I said, "I think I see the flux capacitor from the movie Back to the Future!" I searched on Google and found that the movie gives an awesome example of revelation. Doc says, "It was a revelation, a vision, a picture in my head." The revelation that Doc had of the flux capacitor gave him the idea for his invention. This is perfect wording of how God gives revelation. He can give a revelation by a vision or just a picture in your imagination. This is God speaking to you.

Many people miss God because they don't realize that some of the pictures in their imagination can be from Him. I have missed God in the past before I came to the realization that He gave me pictures in my mind. If I had known that God spoke that way and that it was Him, I would have listened; yet, God patiently waited for me to receive His revelations. At the same time, without being filled with the Holy Spirit, my revelation from God was a slow drip. With the Holy Spirit, my revelation flows more often. When we are filled with the Holy Spirit, we get an upgrade on hearing from God. Where there is no revelation, people cast off restraint; but, blessed is the one who heeds wisdom's instruction (Proverbs 29:18).

When you start to get revelation often, God will allow you to use it to encourage others. God gave me a picture of his love pouring out into His children from above, and then showed me that His love springs forth like living water from our bellies. It comes from God and then goes out to others through giving them encouraging words or having revelation for them.

On the last and greatest day of the festival, Jesus stood and said in a loud voice, "Let anyone who is thirsty come to me and drink. Whoever believes in me, as Scripture has said, rivers of living water will flow from within them." By this he meant the Spirit, whom those who believed in him were later to receive. Up to that time the Spirit had not been given, since Jesus had not yet been glorified. John 7:37-39

This is one of the greatest things ever. "Whoever believes in me, as the Scripture has said, 'Out of his heart will flow rivers of living water'" (John 7:38). Do you feel like you have rivers of living water flowing out of you? When we are filled with the Holy Spirit, the joy for encouraging others in Christ is so amazing that we feel as though living waters are flowing out of us. We are so full with God's love when we read the Word, pray in the Spirit and talk to God.

Our hearts have spiritual eyes. In Ephesians 1:19 Paul shares, "I pray the eyes of your heart would be enlightened." God gives His precious children eyes to see and ears to hear what He has to say to us. This is revelation from God. God showed me that those that are not filled with the Holy Spirit have heart eyes that are almost blind. A baby bird starts out with eyes that are blind, and then one day he begins to see. I was almost blind at one time, but I was content because I didn't know that I was almost blind. Can you imagine an almost blind Christian having the Sword and attacking the enemy but not knowing where to attack? Some people are just stabbing their Sword, The Bible, into the air hoping that they will hit him. When we are filled with the Holy Spirit, we learn to walk in sync with the Holy Spirit so we know what to pray. Our spiritual eyes are enlightened and become in tune to the plans of God's heart and perfect will.

If you pray to be filled with the Holy Spirit, and you do not receive tongues for a long time for whatever reason, know that you were filled with the Holy Spirit when you prayed for it. Tongues are just a manifestation of being filled with the Holy Spirit. If you believe in faith that you were filled with the Holy Spirit when you prayed, then you are. God will move to give you tongues when the time is right. Again, we can't put God in a box. He will move however He chooses.

If we are filled with the Holy Spirit, we have to be in the Word of God. I have definitely been guilty of forgetting to get in the Word in the past. To be filled with the Spirit without reading the Word is a formula for a train wreck. If we have the Spirit, we have to be in the Word daily because the Word will guide us into all truth. When I got filled with the Holy Spirit, God's Word also came alive to me. Pages and pages of the Word that were once one dimensional became two dimensional for me as the Spirit just poured out revelation as I read. It really changed my life in a great way.

God told me the following verse dozens of times in one day.

> "'In the last days, God says, I will pour out my Spirit on all people. Your sons and daughters will prophesy, your young men will see visions, your old men will dream dreams." Acts 2:17

I asked the Lord what this verse meant. The Lord confirmed to me that He is pouring out His Spirit right now. This is one reason why we are on the brink of revival. If you have not prayed to be filled with the Holy Spirit, spend time with the Lord and ask Him to fill you with the Holy Spirit. Talk with the Lord about how you feel about this topic. Being filled with the Holy Spirit is going to help you by giving you the power you need to walk in the Spirit.

Chapter 4

Now Is The Time To Overcome The Wilderness

Just as Jesus was coming out of the water, He saw heaven being torn open and the Spirit descending on him like a dove. And a voice came from heaven, "You are my Son, whom I love; with you I am well pleased." At once the Spirit sent Him out into the wilderness, and He was in the wilderness forty days, being tempted by Satan. He was with the wild animals, and angels attended Him. Mark 1:10-13

The Spirit sent Jesus straight into the wilderness after He was filled with the Holy Spirit. Not all people experience a wilderness season right after they get filled with Holy spirit, so I am not saying that you have to experience this right away. You may have already experienced a wilderness season. You may not have to experience it again. I do want you to be cautious and notice that the first thing the Spirit did to Jesus was to lead Him into the wilderness. We may be led into the wilderness as well. If we stick with Jesus, the person who passed His wilderness test with flying colors, we will do well.

I would love to share some of my wilderness testimony. If sharing my story can in anyway spare you what I went through, then it is worth it. When I got filled with the Holy Spirit, my life turned upside down for good. One week I began praying to the Lord for hours through the night. I needed a breakthrough, and I decided that I was going to pray until I got it. That week was the most amazing week. My elderly neighbor gave her life to Jesus. God healed a little girl from having seizures at a church He asked me to visit. Almost every day something amazing happened. The enemy was sitting there, just waiting. It didn't take long until I struggled with the sin of pride. I mean, "Hey, God was using me!" I fell flat on my face with pride, and the enemy was ready for me. I went through a very painful pride sifting. When you get filled with the Holy Spirit, I recommend that you pray that God "gently" heals you of all prideful strongholds or wrong thoughts that you may have. One thing I learned was not to share anything spiritual that God did through me in order to feel loved by someone else. If you feel very loved when you share something spiritual that you've experienced, there is a good chance this is pride, or a need for love from people. Thankfully God can completely heal His children of this. God has healed me, and I no longer share things in order to feel loved by someone else. Sometimes I have to walk this healing out, and I realize if I should share something with someone. I now share it if God wants me to share it and my story encourages someone in some way. Now that I am healed and that is not a big struggle for me, God actually has me share my testimony quite often. I noticed that people who grew up in a more critical environment struggle with the opposite. They want to hide and not share their story in the event that someone may criticize them for what they say. They may need to practice stepping out more often and realize that it only matters what God thinks. People may always criticize what you say, but you can get to a point where this does not bother you. There may always be a critic.

There are many Christians in America with a lot of knowledge. One of the most important things I can leave with you is for you to understand that knowledge is good, but only if you take action in love. Knowledge is important but should not be the most important thing in life. Knowledge puffs up (1 Corinthians 8:1). We want to be very careful that feeling smart does not result in pride.

Pride is deceptive because it's rarely detected by its owner, and it will steal your life calling. There is a point where you have to ask God to take your head knowledge of Him and drop it down to your heart. Just like we need eyes to see with our heart, we need to love with our heart. For people with a busy doer type personality, it might be harder to grasp this concept but it can be done. We need to ask the Holy Spirit what He would like us to do. Following God's direction in one thing is more significant than doing twenty things for your church that God never intended for you to do. When we agree with God on things, we start to see His heart. When we see how His heart is, then our heart begins to follow suit.

I am not saying that we don't need knowledge. God says, "My people go into exile for a lack of knowledge" (Isaiah 5:13). I definitely went into my wilderness season because I did not have enough knowledge about spiritual warfare. That is one reason I was motivated to write this book. If we use our knowledge and bring it down to our heart, to love others more than to seek approval for ourselves, then we begin to truly know how to love. Our motives become pure in heart. There is a humility that comes with going through trials in life that can be more precious than being the smartest person in the world. A humble person has a teachable spirit. God can use a person who has humility in his or her heart. God resists the proud, but gives grace to the humble (James 4:6). If we look in the Bible, God didn't always use the smartest people. The world focuses on the smartest and most famous people, but God uses the people who are humble in heart. Many times in the Bible, God had to humble people Himself before He could use them. This can be a painful experience.

During my wilderness season I learned about humility. It was one of the hardest seasons of my life. The Lord had to pull my desire to please people out, and then teach me to please Him. I began to realize the root of why I did things. When you start to see the root of things, this is discernment. There is natural discernment and there is spiritual discernment. Spiritual discernment or the gift of discernment is when the Holy Spirit shows you something about someone. It may be the root of why they do something. It is to pray for them. It is never to criticize, gossip, or judge them. You may also begin to discern your own sin. As God reveals it to you, He can heal you.

Peter had a pride sifting when He denied Christ three times (Mark 14:66-72). Jesus was able to restore Peter by asking him if he loved Him three times. Your weakness may not be pride. You may have another weakness. The enemy will look to attack you in all your weak spots. Seek God for healing in any area that you might need. The enemy knew that the Lord was going to use me in the area of setting people free or deliverance. I can't even begin to explain the confusion and attack on my mind during my wilderness season. The enemy also isolated me and told me that I could not tell anyone what I was going through. Some call this the dark night of the soul. After five months of isolation, the Lord told me that He created the body of Christ for a reason and I needed to tell someone what was going on. He asked me to ask a pastor's wife at a different church to mentor me. She ended up mentoring me once a week for over a year.

Here are a few things that will help to bring a breakthrough in a wilderness season.

1. **Stay in the Word**- Reading the Bible daily is very important. The Lord asked me to give someone a Bible

once and reading it helped her break through her depression.

2. **Fasting-** I have learned that fasting for a day or two can help me hear God's voice and bring healing. You can do a Daniel fast, a water fast, or even fast from something instead of food, like technology.

3. **Worshiping God**- Dancing to God around your room and praising God can bring a breakthrough. Praise God when you worship. Be thankful for something in your life, and praise God for it.

4. **Pray for Emotional Release**- Many times I have seen people healed by God when they had an emotional release from something that was holding them back. This is an intercession strategy. Pray it, and you may see God do a mighty work in your life.

5. **Put on the Full Armor of God**- Read the Word. Put on your under armour- pray in the Spirit.

6. **Rebuking Satan**- Rebuke things that you discern can help. Sometimes if I discern something, I can rebuke it and then the enemy leaves and the lie behind it surfaces. The power of Jesus in you causes the enemy to flee. Jesus told Satan to go at the end of His wilderness time. He said "Be gone," and Satan left. Sometimes it's good to tell the Enemy to "Be gone!"

7. **Pray for God's Protection**- Pray the blood of Jesus over your life and your loved ones. Pray for God to send angels to help and protect you. In Mark 1:13, Jesus had angels to protect Him.

8. **Soaking Prayer**- There are some times where we may feel stuck and we need a breakthrough to hear

God's voice. Soaking is a good strategy for this time. Soaking is when you play worship music and you pray and worship God. Another strategy God taught me if you feel stuck, is to dance around your house to worship music. This may be a little out of your comfort zone, but it really helps.

9. **Pray Scripture**- "For the word of God is alive and active. Sharper than any double-edged sword, it penetrates even to dividing soul and spirit, joints and marrow; it judges the thoughts and attitudes of the heart" (Hebrews 4:12).

Praying scripture is a very powerful offensive weapon against the enemy. The Bible is one of the most powerful positive forces in the world. Hebrews 4:12 says, the Word "is sharper than a double-edged sword." One morning, God told me that He was going to give me a new strategy to help pray for the people I love. God then began to show me that praying scripture is very powerful. He specifically had me insert people's names into the verses. For example, my oldest sons name is Landon. I began to pray, "Landon is patient, Landon is kind. Landon does not envy, he does not boast, he is not proud. Landon does not delight in evil but rejoices in the truth." I am not joking I saw all kinds of miracles in my family after I prayed scripture. It was amazing! Speaking scripture over ourselves allows God to use the Sword of the Spirit to break through in areas where we need help in our lives. It is one of the best things to do in a wilderness season as well because it is an offensive weapon against the enemy. I usually ask

God what verse He wants me to use. If I am praying scripture for others, I also look at what they are going through and try to find verses that relate to these areas. Beth Moore has a great book called *Praying God's Word*. This book can help you find great scriptures to go with different struggles. I have it downloaded on my iPhone in case I need a quick reference. If you are anxious, you can look up verses on anxiety and pray your name in those verses. Place your name in the blanks in the following verses.

"I _____ will cast my cares on the Lord for he cares for me" (1 Peter 5:7).

"I _____ am not anxious about anything but with everything with prayer and petition with thanksgiving present my requests to God" (Philippians 4:6).

If you are struggling with a sin or stronghold, you can pray: "If the son has set me free, I am free indeed" (John 8:36).

When I am struggling with my identity I like to pray, "I am my beloved's and his desire is for me" (Song of Solomon 7:10).

It is very important to pray the verses out loud. This gives them authority in the spiritual realm.

Pray with me: Lord, deliver us from our wilderness season. Set us free. Give us emotional release and heal our deepest wounds. I pray every word spoken against us null and void. We submit our hearts to you.

Chapter 5
Now Is The Time to Know Our Identity

And a voice from heaven said, "This is my Son, whom I love; with him I am well pleased."
Matthew 3:17

Before Jesus went into the wilderness, God spoke a promise over Him. He spoke His identity over Him. He told Him that He loved Him and that He was pleased with Him. These are two things that I feel are very important to know. We must know that God loves us and that He is proud of us. This is a very important part of our identity in Christ. Jesus needed to hear this from God before He went into the wilderness, and I believe we need to hear and remember this, especially during our wilderness season.

A major battle that the enemy wants to have over us is identity theft. He wants to come and steal our identity so that we don't remember who we are in Christ. If he can do this, then we are left weak and wandering in the wilderness. God will gently remind us of who we are. The enemy attacks who I am in Christ anytime He can. He does not want me to know who I am and that I am a child of God. I know that sometimes I am very hard on myself. Maybe I didn't get enough done during the day or I wasted time. I begin to feel guilt or shame. Then God shows me that He is proud of me and that I am doing my best.

My friend Brandie was praying for someone and God showed her a picture. She saw the girl she was praying for. The girl was looking into the mirror and saw a very ugly face. This was the way that she saw herself. Then God showed her the other side of the mirror. She was beautiful. God saw her as she was on the other side, a beautiful child of God. He loves her just the way she is and doesn't need her to be someone that she is not.

If our identity is in our ministry it is on shaking sand. When our identity is in God, He gives us the desires of our hearts. We almost have to give up on our dream initially because we have to give up doing it our way. Then God may give our dream back so we can do it God's way. We have to move out of the way so it's all God. God's strength is made perfect in our weakness (2 Corinthians 12:9).

We tend to beat ourselves up sometimes for our mistakes and for our sin. If God is revealing hidden sin to us, it's because He loves us and He wants us to confess it. The Bible says the Lord corrects those He loves (Hebrews 12: 6-11). If we have the ability to hear His voice and His correction, that means we are in the right place. We can confess our sin and with God's help, move on.

We also have to be careful of getting under the law. This is a huge attack from the enemy. Galatians 5:18 says, "But if you are led by the Spirit, you are not under the law." I grew up in a family that was full of grace. As far as I knew, I never struggled with the law until I ended up in my wilderness season. If you are feeling numb towards God and you feel like you are constantly having to strive to earn His love, you might be under the law. Grace says you are covered by love.

"It is for freedom that Christ has set us free. Stand firm, then, and do not let yourselves be burdened again by a yoke of slavery. Mark my words! I, Paul, tell you that if you let yourselves be circumcised, Christ will be of no value to you at all. Again I declare to every man who lets himself be circumcised that he is obligated to obey the whole law. You who are trying to be justified by the law have been alienated from Christ; you have fallen away from grace. For through the Spirit we eagerly await by faith the righteousness for which we hope." Galatians 5:1-5

There is nothing more numbing than falling away from grace. We have to eagerly await by faith what is promised to us. We are validated by the righteousness for which we hope. If we get into a legalistic mindset, we can forget that we are righteous. We never have to earn God's love. There are groups of Christians that believe they have to earn their way to heaven. This is a legalistic mindset or a religious spirit. When I struggled with this mindset, I watched a Martin Luther video. I saw the struggle he had with the religious spirit or the need to earn his way to heaven. Martin Luther broke through the religious spirit and found freedom in Christ. He found the grace of Jesus Christ. If you feel this way, I pray that God would set you free from the law and that you would fall into His arms of grace.

You are valuable. You are chosen. You are dearly loved. I pray that you would know your identity in Christ and that it would stick. I pray the enemy will not be able to steal your identity.

Pray with me:
God show me how much You love me and how You see me, place my identity firmly in You.

What is God saying to your heart?

_____

_____

_____

_____

_____

_____

_____

_____

_____

Chapter 6

Now Is The Time for Purity

Blessed are the pure in heart, for they will see God.
Matthew 5:8

Do you ever struggle with needing to be perfect? No one is perfect. Being perfect is very different than being pure. In our society, many people struggle with needing to be perfect, but God does not call us to be perfect; He calls us to be pure. If we have accepted Jesus as our savior, our sins are covered with God's righteousness. A person who is pure, but not perfect, realizes that if they confess their sin before God, they are wiped clean. They can confess their sins and move on. Since Jesus is the mediator between God and man, we can confess directly to Him. A dependent spirit needs to confess their sins to a third party, such as a priest, or have someone else pray for them. Although I do not judge people who do this, I do pray they would realize that we can walk in freedom if we confess directly to Jesus.

The enemy may try to attack you and make you inward-focused. Someone that is inward-focused may dwell on their sin for a long time even though God says that He remembers it no more. This is a normal strategy of the enemy to convince you that your sins are not forgiven. This could be a legalistic or religious spirit telling you this. If this is you, God is gracious to heal you, help you move on, and help you focus more on loving others.

If we want to walk in new levels with God, then we have to strive for a life of purity. This does not mean that we won't sin. It means that we have a healthy understanding that when we do make a mistake, God is faithful to forgive us when we ask Him. The purer your heart is, the more sensitive you are to God's voice. There is a purity that comes when we are responsive to the Holy Spirit nudging us to change. Sometimes we tend to justify things in our lives as okay when they are not. God is a God of love and He will gently help us with these things.

Can you imagine a person who is studying to become a pastor and they lie and cheat on an application? This is something that they justify as okay because they need to go to school so it would be best to lie just a little. If God cannot trust us with small things, then He cannot trust us with larger things. I pray that you would look at the problematic things in your life that may seem justified, but deep down you know that they are not right.

One thing God showed me was that I justified

some things as okay in someone else's life because I loved this person. The Bible tells us that we are supposed to follow the rules of the land. Many people, see a stop sign but read it as, "Stop, except for you." They roll right through it. Yet the stop sign is there for our safety. I know when God really started telling me that He wanted me to go to new levels with Him, one of the first things He corrected was my driving. We have to live a pure life, even in the little things, if we want God to use us for bigger things.

If we want to go to new levels with God, He usually starts making us pure by correcting little things in our lives that we may have justified as okay. He may start with our driving. We are going to be called to a higher standard than we used to because the enemy will be looking for cracks in our life to squeeze through. God will be looking to seal all these cracks. We don't want to go into ministry with cracks in our lives.

My dad was the best example to me that everyone is called to ministry in their daily lives, not just pastors. My dad was constantly fixing things for our widowed neighbors and anyone who needed help. He flowed with a helps ministry and truly cared about everyone he came in contact with. I love defining ministry as living a legacy to love others and to help them.

Sometimes we will need to know what God is asking us to change or do. God may have something He is asking you to do or He may be asking you not to do something. It may be something that no one else has to do. There are some things that I cannot do that other people can, but God has made it clear to me that He doesn't want me to do them. When God shows us things that He wants us to change, I've learned that I need to write them down. Writing down what He speaks to me is a huge key to my freedom. If I have it written down, I can look back and remember what He said and reflect on His guidance when needed.

God has clearly asked me not to dredge up the past. This is a huge key to my freedom. It's not healthy. He only has me look at my past when He shows me it and He wants to give me a deeper healing. He is usually the one to bring it up to me. I try not to do the things that God has asked me not to do. I don't do them because I love God and I want to keep my freedom in Christ. When I do them and have a small relapse, I quickly remember what the days of my wilderness were like, and I confess my sin and turn away. Then I get in the Word and in prayer so that God can sort it all out. Then, I speak out that I am free in Christ, and I walk in my freedom.

Let's look at two versions of Galatians 5:16: "I say then: Walk in the Spirit, and you shall not fulfill the lust of the flesh." (NKJV) and "So I say, let the Holy Spirit guide your lives. Then you won't be doing what your sinful nature craves." (NLT) If you start to walk in the flesh, just confess your sin and try again. If you are a Christian, know that your sins are covered by Christ's blood when you confess them. God will help you continue to walk in the Spirit.

God's rules are different than the world's rules. The media says sex is not sacred. They act like it's a casual kiss. However, we give someone a piece of our soul when we have sex with them. Maybe you are having sex outside of marriage; God made this rule to protect us. There are prayers to break off soul ties if you have sex before you are married. God can also redeem your heart and soul, but you have to make a change when He convicts you. When God shows you these things, it's okay. He will help you come up with a plan to help you make a change. God can forgive you if you have done things in the past. Just ask Him for forgiveness. You may still have consequences, but your sin is erased in God's mind as He forgives you. However, if you want to go through the wilderness, the best way to do this is to justify sin as being okay. The best way to get out of the wilderness is to ask God to help you stay pure. I pray that God would create a pure heart within us and help us to stay focused on Him.

Is there any area that you feel that God may want you to seek more purity in? If so, give this area to the Lord, and ask Him to help you make it pure. You may need to take some steps by doing what God asks you to do to have more freedom. Sometimes God asks us to break ties with people who we know may cause us to stumble. You will walk in great freedom after you break the ties. If God asks you to give up someone or a group of people, He will eventually replace them with someone else or another group that is even better for you.

Pray with me:

Lord, reveal any area of our lives where we need to walk in a deeper level of purity and help us to turn away from the things that you do not want us to do. Help us to know that the reward will be great because you say the pure in heart will see you.

What is God saying to your heart about purity?

_____
_____
_____
_____
_____
_____
_____
_____
_____
_____
_____
_____
_____
_____
_____
_____
_____
_____

Chapter 7

Now Is The Time to Worship

"But the time is coming--indeed it's here now--when true worshipers will worship the Father in spirit and in truth. The Father is looking for those who will worship him that way."   John 4:23-24 (NLT)

Do you want to be a true worshiper? True worshipers worship in spirit and in truth. Sara Nicholls, a worship leader at Engaging Heaven Church in Connecticut, is an expert on worshiping. She says that worshiping in spirit is worshiping in surrender. It is giving God all your idols and laying them down at His feet. Sara also shares that worshiping in truth is worshiping in obedience.

Worship isn't just singing to God at church on Sunday. Worship is a lifestyle. Worship is reading God's word and praying in the Spirit. Worship is loving others with the love of God. When I first got filled with the Spirit, I heard stories of people who went to the secret place of their prayer closet alone with God for hours and hours, sometimes even all day long. I thought,

"How could this be?" I was lucky if I could focus on God for 10-30 minutes in prayer. Then I realized that by praying God's Word and praying in the Spirit over people, God will reveal His heart (the gift of prophecy) on how to pray for others. The life of an intercessor takes on a whole new meaning. It becomes a time in our prayer closets to fight the enemy for ourselves, our families, and other people. It's absolutely amazing! The first time I prayed like this, I was praying for someone, and I got a reel of about 10 pictures in my mind. There were so many pictures that I was overwhelmed and I had no idea what to do. I definitely did not remember them all. I realized that God is patient with me. I began to write down the pictures that I saw, and I asked God what they meant. With practice, I am now able to pray for the pictures in my mind as I see them and then move on to the next one. God may speak differently to you. Don't feel like He has to speak to you in the same way that He speaks to me. He may have a special and unique way to speak to you.

We need to be careful not to worship for show. I think the enemy uses the distraction that others are watching us to hinder us from thinking about God. I've trained myself to let all those thoughts drop out of my mind and not care what others think of me. Then, I can truly get into a heart of worship. Some people may worship at church by singing and praying in tongues. Right after the verse where God commands us to be filled with the Spirit, He says to sing to each other with songs from the Spirit (Ephesians 5: 19). This does not bother me when someone sings in the Spirit, but we need to make sure that however we worship, our motive is not to impress others. I think this is one of the main reasons why Paul addresses tongues and creates rules for them in the church. I can't imagine 50 different people trying to speak in tongues at the same time. That would be crazy!

Worshiping God is a very important part of our lives. I love worship. Sometimes when I am singing to God and blessing Him, I can hear Him speak to me and there are many times that the words He says to me are exactly what I need to hear at that time. The words from God are very healing to my soul. The Word says "man shall not live on bread alone but on every word that comes out of the mouth of God" (Matthew 4:4). Now is the time for Christians to learn to rely on God's voice. His perfect *rhema* word will satisfy our soul.

I love it when I'm really trusting God and I have a good worship song in my heart and mind all day long. I love it when I am worshiping the Lord for all that He has done. Worship may look different for you than for someone else. Worship may be dancing in your room, praying and singing to God, reading your Bible out loud by singing scripture, or even just reading scripture. Spending time with God can be a form of worship. You can ask God how He wants you to worship. He might love for you to worship Him anyway that you want.

God can use a song to usher in His presence powerfully. God is even uses secular songs to do this. The Christian world view reveals that you can find God in almost everything. He can speak to you through anything He wants. Sara Nicolls shares how she sang a song in high school to try out for a play and God moved so mightily through her song that when she was done everyone was captivated and people were crying. As we discover God's heart, we have our eyes opened to see God's presence through music. God uses people in the area of music to display His presence. Jordan Smith was used by God on The Voice. God is calling Jordan to usher in God's presence through his singing for such a time as this. Adam Levine even said that he believed that God signed Jordan's voice, meaning God autographed it. My friend Bria Blessing is being used by God in the Ukraine as a singer to give them hope as well. I love to laugh with my friends because God speaks to me often through popular pop songs. One of my favorite songs is Charlie Puth's song "One Call Away." The words are powerful. I love knowing that God is only one call away. There is something about God releasing His power through a song that is so moving and undeniable.

We were all created to worship. Whether we know it or not, we are either worshiping Jesus or worshiping something else.

God inhabits the praises of His people. When we enter His gates with thanksgiving in our hearts and enter His courts with praise, it is a sweet aroma to God (Psalm 100:4). When we are joyful in our circumstances, we are also worshiping God. Have you ever had a child that naturally complained and another child that was naturally thankful? I've had this, and I just want to lavish blessing onto the one that is thankful. I may have to work a little harder to bless the un-thankful child, and I might have to let them go through harder times a little longer until he is more thankful. In the same way, being thankful is worship to God's ears.

Praise God and thank Him for all that He has given you. If you need to confess an unthankful heart, go ahead and do this now. God is full of mercy and grace. Ask God to show you the best way that you can worship Him. Is there a place that you love being alone with God? Go to this place and spend time worshiping Him.

What is God saying to your heart about worship?

_____

_____

_____

_____

_____

_____

_____

_____

_____

_____

_____

_____

_____

_____

_____

Chapter 8

Now Is The Time to Follow God's Lead (Obey God)

Jesus gave them this answer: "Very truly I tell you, the Son can do nothing by himself; he can do only what he sees his Father doing, because whatever the Father does the Son also does."   John 5:19

Obeying God is a form of worship. Romans 12:1 says, "Therefore, I urge you, brethren, by the mercies of God, to present your bodies a living and holy sacrifice, acceptable to God, which is your spiritual service of worship." A secret to walking in step with the Spirit is to ask God what you should do to obey Him. A lot of Christians volunteer and do a lot of things in the church; yet, we do not always stop to ask God what He wants us to do. Do you feel burned out? If so, this could be you.

God longs for us to go to Him and ask Him what He wants us to do. If we have a relationship with our Father, we can go to Him and spend time with Him and ask Him what He wants us to do anytime we want.

Instead of doing many things in our church and being burned out, God might want us to do one thing really well. We just need to ask Him. The most amazing days in my life have occurred when I woke up in the morning and I asked God, "What do you want me to do today? Help me to walk in the Spirit." Following God's Spirit for what He has in mind for my day allows me to be in step with His will.

I remember one time when I asked God what church He wanted me to go to the next day. We were visiting churches at the time. God began to bring to my mind a certain church's website when I was online. I felt Him say that He wanted me to go there. I went the next morning. My children were with some family members, and I ended up going by myself. During worship, a friend invited me to come down to the front where everyone was standing. I went about half way and then told her that I wanted to stop there because I didn't want to be right in the front. I thanked her, and I stood near another friend while we worshiped. Out of nowhere, my friend's daughter began to have a seizure. She fell directly into her mother's arms and into my arms. We were both holding her, and I just began to pray in my mind by myself. After about 20 seconds, the girl was still having a seizure and the Holy Spirit rose up inside me, and I prayed, "God heal her" and "I believe that you will." Immediately she stood up and stopped having the seizure, and she looked completely normal. They took her to the side, and I went over to check on her and told her that I felt like she was going to be just fine. After church her family took her to the ER, and the ER doctors said, "She didn't have a seizure; she has no signs of having a seizure." They assured her that she did have one, but the ER doctors said, "No, she did not." There were no signs because God had healed her! A few years later I was able to share this story with the little girl's mom, and she said that they had seizures in their family history and she felt like God was showing her that He had healed her daughter of seizures for good. Praise God!

Asking God where He wants us is very powerful. It allows Him to use us as a vessel wherever He wants us. A lot of times we tend to want God to work in the way we want Him to work or to bless us in the way we want Him to. Asking God to bless us is a very good thing, but maybe we need to ask Him where He wants us.

God may ask you to do something. I had a dream one time that I had an assignment in a very rough neighborhood while Jenn Hatmaker had an assignment in a very fancy neighborhood. A few days later, Jenn announced that HGTV was going to be taping her family on a home remodeling show. I later had another dream to look online where I found a job to tutor students who had been kicked out of their school and were in an alternative program. I interviewed and got the job. A lot of people asked me why would I want to teach there and why would I not want to teach at a nicer school. I told them that I loved it, and I would not want to teach anywhere else because it was where I was called. This job was actually easy for me because I had an anointing to do it. The kids were amazing, and because I had them one-on-one, I was able to really touch their lives. They were so thankful that someone cared for them that they may have touched my life just as much as I touched theirs.

If God gives you an assignment, He will give you an anointing to do it. Whether it's in a fancy area or in a lower income area, you will love doing what God has called you to do. You can ask God to give you an assignment. Matthew 7:7 says, "Ask and it shall be given unto you, seek and you shall find, knock and the door shall be open unto you." I believe that we need to pray prophetically in God's will to hear God's assignments for our lives. I love to pray for assignments from the Lord. There is nothing more fulfilling than an assignment from Him because He puts you right where you are supposed to be. One morning when I woke up, I saw a picture of a desk with five folders on it. The Lord said that those were five assignments that He had for me. As I prayed about, it God showed me what they were. The number five is also symbolic of grace, and the Lord has been teaching me to have grace for myself and others. Pray for God to give you assignments from Him. We need assignments from God, not assignments from men.

I had an elderly neighbor in Connecticut named Mr. Mike. I took care of him on the weekends. He was not a Christian. His wife accepted Christ, and he was very skeptical. I really liked him, and I always prayed for him. One day he fell in his home. This caused him to have to go into a rehab center. I felt led by the Lord to go by and visit him one morning. On the way in, I felt the Lord nudge me to take my Bible. When I got to his room, he wanted something to read. I had a magazine, so I gave it to him. Then he wanted something else to read. I handed him my Bible. He took a church bulletin out of it and read, "Jesus is the risen Lord and savior." He nodded his head and said, "Yes." Again he said, "Jesus is the risen Lord and savior." He nodded his head and said, "Yes" again. I got a call the next day that Mr. Mike passed away that night in his sleep. I prayed and felt God say that he had become a Christian, and he was proclaiming it with me that day. I went back to the rehab center to see his wife, and the people who worked there said that one day he was suddenly very open to going to the church there and he learned about God. I was amazed at what God had done for Mr. Mike. Romans says, "If you confess with your mouth that Jesus is Lord and believe in your heart that God raised him from the dead, you will be saved" (Romans 10:9). This is what Mr. Mike did.

When we start asking God what He wants us to do, we learn to walk in the Spirit wherever the Spirit leads us. I had a friend who was moving to a new house. One day she prayed in desperation for someone to help her pack. At the time I was praying, and the Lord led me to scroll through texts on my phone. I saw her text message, and I suddenly felt her worry and stress. I texted her to see if she needed any help packing. She was shocked, and she told me that I could come help her. When I arrived, she told me about her prayer. Her spirit prayed to the Holy Spirit, and the Holy Spirit spoke to me about her need. When we walk in step with the Spirit, God can use us to help others and further the Kingdom of God.

Sometimes God may ask you not to do something. There was one time when God asked me not to go to church. I thought, "Really? Why would God not want me to go to church?" There was some snow that day, and I thought maybe He wanted me to stay safe. I decided to pray for His protection from the snow and then I went. At church someone gave me a small pamphlet that I read. The pamphlet had skewed beliefs that caused me to have pride. It took me a few years to get healed. If I had obeyed God, I would not have had this struggle. In hindsight, I should have stopped and asked God why He didn't want me to go to church. I learned a valuable lesson to obey God's voice even when it doesn't make sense to me.

David Hogan, a cowboy missionary in Mexico, speaks of a time when God told him to turn right while driving. He went right and later found out that the Mexican cartel had a huge ambush and killed everyone that went the way he usually would have gone had he turned left. Learning to hear God's voice can not only bless you, but it can also save you a lot of heartache. In the times we are living in, we have to be able to hear God's voice and know that it's Him speaking. We will also need His strength to obey Him. God never makes us obey Him; He allows us to choose to obey.

Do you follow God's lead? Ask God what was the last thing He asked you to do. This is a great strategy. Doug Addison often talks about the fact that sometimes God is waiting patiently for us to do the last thing He asked us to do so He can move us on to something else. Ask God if there is anything that He has asked you to do that you may have forgotten about. If He tells you something, write it down so you won't forget. Go back and do what the Lord has asked you to do. He can help you if you need the strength to do it.

What is God saying to your heart?

_____

_____

_____

_____

_____

_____

_____

_____

_____

_____

_____

_____

_____

_____

_____

Chapter 9

Now Is The Time To Humble Ourselves

Humble yourselves, therefore, under God's mighty hand, that he may lift you up in due time.
1 Peter 5:6

Is it prideful to want to be used by God? The answer to this question depends on your heart motive. One of Satan's biggest attacks is to get us inward-focused so that we can't think about anything but needing to be used by God. If the enemy can do this, he can get us to have pride by looking for ways God can use us in order to feel validated. This heart motive is to advance our godly reputation or feel loved by preforming for the approval of others.

I had an adventure a few years ago. The Spirit inside of me said, "God use me," as I was driving. I didn't say it. I heard it. Then I exited on the wrong exit or so I thought. I went to make a u-turn when I heard God's voice say, "Go right, go left, see that

McDonald's? Turn in here, and look over there. I ended up at a liquor store. I sat in the car wondering if God would want me to go into a liquor store. Just about that time I thought, "Sure He would;" Jesus turned water into wine. I was having a celebration dinner for my husband because he was finishing his first year of his PhD, so I decided to go inside and get some wine. I went inside, and I immediately noticed that the owner and his wife were there with their children. I overheard the mother say that her younger son was an accident and he never obeyed. She said that she wished she had never had him, and he was standing right next to her and could hear her. I could see the distress in his spirit as he tried to do everything he could do to please his mom, but nothing was good enough. I asked the Lord what He wanted me to do, and felt that I was to intercede for this child. I prayed in faith believing that God would help his mom realize what she was doing and that she would accept her child and love him for who he was. I prayed she would realize that he was not a mistake. Then, I bought wine, said hello to the boy, smiled at him, and left. I just knew in my heart that the boy was praying to God and that God sent me there to pray for him. This whole adventure was solely for God's glory.

A few weeks later, I prayed on my own for God to use me. I immediately felt a cold chill and a disconnect from God. It felt very wrong. So I immediately prayed "never mind" and to reverse the prayer. I prayed that God would show me if it was wrong to pray that prayer because something did not feel right about praying it. This was my gift of discernment showing me that something was wrong. God showed me that He wanted me to seek Him on this for a while. For a long time, it felt wrong when I prayed this prayer.

One day, God showed me the answer. God showed me that I wanted Him to use me to earn some kind of spiritual badge. I wanted to feel special. I wanted to feel godly. I had the ugly "p" word again: pride. The whole purpose of the Kingdom of God is to allow God to further His glory. It didn't matter if He used me. He could use someone else. That would be okay. When I am a vessel and I move out of the way, it allows the Holy Spirit to take the credit. If He wants to use me, yes, I am ready and willing; but if He wants to use someone else, that's fine too. It's all for His glory. We should be able to get to a point where we no longer need to advance our godly reputations. This is a performance for man and not for God. If we are not full of the Holy Spirit, we may be full of a religious spirit. The religious spirit is performance based. We may feel we need to say the most spiritual thing or do the most spiritual thing in the world to be elevated. When in reality, the most spiritual thing to do might be to give someone who is cold a coat or give someone who is thirsty a glass of water. When we do this in secret with only God knowing, we have a great reward (Matthew 6:1- 4). When we ask God to heal us, He begins to reveal our heart motives to us, and as we cooperate with Him, He heals us.

Jesus made Himself of no reputation. He didn't need to be the most spiritual person in the world, even though He actually was. He would often tell people that He didn't want them to tell anyone that they were healed or set free.

Some people get a need to be elevated for spiritual things as a child by the way they were rewarded with praise for doing something spiritual by their parents. Some people also get this need from their Christian friends as it's "cool" to be spiritual. If you struggle with this, there is hope. Seek healing from the Lord. It starts with a right mindset. God forgave me for the pride of trying to advance my godly reputation.

God, I pray that You will heal us from the need to elevate ourselves.

The Lord says that if we humble ourselves, God will lift us up (1 Peter 5:6). We don't want false humility where we say we are not worth anything. The enemy gives false humility. We need real humility. Real humility says, "I'm going to give God all the credit for this, so I'm not going to post it on Facebook to further my reputation. I am going to share it only if it helps someone." Real humility says, "I am going to do only what I see the Father doing, and I don't need credit for it. I am going to follow God's lead. I don't need to tell everyone all the latest things God has done in my life, all the people I've witnessed to in the last few months, and hope that they will love me more. I am going to humble myself, and God will lift me up."

Is it prideful to ask God to use us? I believe that if our heart motivation has anything to do with our godly reputation, then yes, it is prideful to ask God to use us. If our motivation is not to get credit, but to love others and further the Kingdom of God, then I believe our prayer would look more like this; "God use anyone you want to further your Kingdom, and if it's me, then I am willing." If our heart has the right motive, then we can pray that God will use us for His glory.

Then I heard the voice of the Lord saying, "Whom shall I send? And who will go for us?" And I said, "Here am I. Send me!" Isaiah 6:8

The Lord wants people who are willing to be used by Him, but they must learn to be humble and give Him all the credit. The Lord has given me this verse and told me to sound the alarm and warn His people:

"If my people, who are called by my name, will humble themselves and pray and seek my face and turn from their wicked ways, then I will hear from heaven, and I will forgive their sin and will heal their land."
2 Chronicles 7:14

Now is the time to serve the Lord and not man. Many churches are performance based, and they are preforming for man and not for God. Now is the time that the Lord will heal His Bride the Church. However, He won't force this on anyone. The only churches that will get healed are the ones that are willing to follow God's lead over the lead of the elders and the church board. God may even have the churches who listen to Him change the format of their service. If the Holy Spirit is in charge, He might not always want the service to be in the format of worship and a then a sermon. God is rewiring the church to seek Him instead of the standard worship/ sermon format. Those that change will have revival because they will be in step with God's heart.

Pray with me:
Lord, I pray that you will heal the churches in America and in the World. Help us to serve you and not preform for man. I pray that we would be ignited with your fire to be used for your glory in any way you want to use us. I pray that we would not want credit but would seek to love others and further the Kingdom of God.

What is God saying to your heart?

_____

_____

_____

_____

_____

_____

_____

_____

_____

Chapter 10

Now Is The Time For Prophetic Prayer

"I wish you could all speak in tongues, but even more I wish you could all prophesy. For prophecy is greater than speaking in tongues, unless someone interprets what you are saying so that the whole church will be strengthened." 1 Corinthians 14:5 (NLT)

Have you ever wanted to pray exactly in God's will? Praying exactly in God's will is prophetic prayer. It's amazing! The enemy knows that prophecy is God's heart, and he does not want people to know what God's heart is, so he may give some Christians a fear of prophecy. Prophecy is getting in line with God's perfect will and His heart. I can't imagine anything more wonderful than that! God can give you a special promise for yourself or He can have someone else give you a prophetic word. A prophetic word is a supernatural word from God for someone else. Dennis Cramer, a prophetic speaker, says that everyone who is filled with the Holy Spirit can pray for the gift of prophecy. In the Bible many people prayed in tongues for the first time and then prophesied (Acts 19:7).

One way to get the gift of prophecy is by impartation. Spiritual gifts can be imparted by the laying on of hands. When I am imparting something to someone I usually place my hand on their forehead and pray this prayer, "What I have I give to you, freely as I have received, freely I give" (Matthew 10:8).

There are many ways someone with the gift of prophecy receives revelation from God. One way is that people get actual words from God to give to other people. They may have words literally drop into their spirit, and they say them and think that they must have come from God. Some people see a word written out in their imagination.

Another type of prophetic gift to encourage the Church is a seeing gift. People with this gift are also known as seers. With this gift, Christians see pictures in their mind and have to ask God what the pictures mean and how they should be interpreted. When a prophetic word is given, it is meant to encourage, edify, and build up the Church. In the New Testament, a prophetic word is never meant to tear down or hurt someone. Seers can also see into the spiritual realm when needed. They may see angels. Any type of prophetic gift is not to advance ourselves but is to help others and further the Kingdom of God.

When prophetic people speak, it is amazing because they usually speak exactly God's words for a group of people. One of my favorite prophets is Dennis

Cramer. He is the most organized prophetic person I have ever seen. I have never seen anyone more right-brained, logical, and prophetic than him. You might want to look him up on YouTube. Everyone loves it when Dennis Cramer prophecies over them because they get an encouraging word from the Lord. However, when he speaks it is amazing because it is God's words.

One time Dennis Cramer shared how a girl raised her hand and said, "Mr. Cramer, I know what you are going to say before you say it." He said "Great, you have caught the prophetic anointing. Go ahead and finish the word." He sat down and let her finish. She was right on with exactly what he was going to say. Does this sound creepy? Not at all. If God has a word for people, then anyone who hears His voice well can share it. I think it shows humility that Dennis Cramer allowed someone else to finish the word for him. He was revealing that he did not need the credit, and he can give God the glory.

The opposite of the prophetic anointing or God's words would be when a pastor doesn't spend time with God and then preaches his own sermon. When this happens, I feel that the words are not from God; they are from man. God can speak through anyone anytime He wants, but it is amazing when someone who is yielding to the Holy Spirit speaks His words. When someone is preaching with a prophetic anointing I usually know. Sometimes God shows me a few pictures during the word before a speaker says them to confirm that the word being spoken is from Him. I remember the first time this happened; I was shocked, but then someone told me what was going on. Now I love when God confirms for me that a word is from Him.

Dreaming is a type of prophetic gift. It is seeing pictures in your mind at night. Dreams can come from three places: the Lord, the enemy, or your soul working things out in your life. All three types of dreams can be interpreted, meaning you can ask God what the dream means. The Holy Spirit will tell you if it's important or not, and if it's symbolic or literal. The Holy Spirit can also tell you what it means. I usually ask God, and if He doesn't tell me right away, He will usually tell me throughout the day at some point. If you see something during the day, you may have a vision or a moving picture. Some of the visions and pictures have actual or literal meaning; they are actually going to happen to you. My friend, Hannah Poe, shared a vision she saw when she tried to conceive for three years. She saw her son. God was giving her a promise that she would have children. Years later she realized that she was in the exact moment of the vision that she saw years before. She had the same clothes on, and her son had the same blond haircut.

Some people call symbolic messages from God dreams and literal messages from God visions, but I do not. I don't want to confuse anyone. If a message is given to me at night, I call it a dream. If a message is given to me while I am awake, I call it a vision.

Another type of dreaming is symbolic dreaming.

You may have this if you see strange things. Have you ever had a dream that you lost a tooth? Have you ever dreamed that you were naked in public? These are symbolic. If you lose a tooth, it usually means that you need wisdom for something. It's a play on words for wisdom teeth. If you were naked in public, it means that God wants you to be honest and vulnerable in front of others. It is very powerful when people are vulnerable and honest because they can relate to other people who are going through the same thing.

I was praying about this book and asked God to show me an encouraging word because the enemy was really attacking me. If the enemy attacks me, then I know that what I am doing is usually something he does not want but God really wants. If the enemy starts attacking me in something, I usually say, "This is going to get good!" God gave me a picture, and I was standing at a welcome desk at a church and I was handing out balloons. God has shown me that balloons are symbolic of the Holy Spirit, and He said that this book would help people who want to be filled with the Spirit. He also showed me a second picture. He was putting an engine into a grocery cart. I thought, "What does that mean, God? I am laughing." I felt Him say that I was going to help people understand how to have the power of the Holy Spirit and most of my readers would be moms who shop at the grocery store. The engine is symbolic of power.

I have the type of prophetic gift that sees pictures. I usually see something very neat and positive and encouraging. Sometimes I have a knowing from Him, deep in my heart, that I am supposed to share it, and sometimes I have to ask God if I am supposed to share it. If I see something negative, I always ask God if I am supposed to share something about it and what it means before I share it. Sometimes God has me use a "flip it" method. Doug Addison shares this strategy for prophecy. It means that I "flip" the negative thing I see to say it in a positive way because God sees the positive in them. Since God is love, and He extends His love and grace to us, He even gives warnings in encouraging ways.

The way in which we deliver a word is very important. We can give a word in an encouraging and loving heart, and someone will receive it well. We can give the same exact word with a critical and negative heart, and the person will not receive it because they feel attacked by the word. I have been given a critical and negative word before, and it was very hard to handle. In the New Testament, prophecy is intended to strengthen, encourage, and comfort (1 Corinthians 14:3). If the word you feel led to give someone does not strengthen or encourage, then you should ask God how you should say it before you give it to someone.

Occasionally God has had me wait to release a word to someone for another time. I once had a dream that I was supposed to tell a couple to stop their ministry, but then the scene changed in the dream and I saw a child. When I was about to share it, God asked me to wait to share the dream. One day, God told me to go ahead and share the dream with them. I sent them a message on Facebook, and they wrote me back saying that they had not told anyone but they had recently found out that they were pregnant for the first time. They were also praying for direction for their ministry. God had me wait to share this in His timing. Learning His timing is a process. It's not always learned instantly. Another time I had a dream that I would impart the gift of prophecy into the Baptists. In the dream I laid hands on my old Baptist youth pastor, John Durham, and imparted the gift or prophecy to him. This was very exciting to me! When you walk with God and get a full prophetic revelation from Him, life is one exciting adventure. Puzzle pieces fall together and God ties themes together. Being in step with God's will allows all kinds of romantic, exciting adventures. He definitely satisfies a longing heart with relationship and loving others with His amazing power! You can ask God for the gift of prophecy and all the gifts of the Spirit. Anyone who has prayed to be filled with the Holy Spirit can prophesy over someone else; it just takes practice. A good place to start practicing is in a prayer group.

When you get a prophetic word or promise from God, you may sometimes see the opposite happening at first in the natural realm. This is because Satan is furious. You will need to have faith to walk out the promise that God has given you. You will need to walk by faith and not by sight. When you do this, your promise or word from God will come to pass.

One of our Compassion children wrote us the

following nugget of wisdom, and it blew me away.
"When people lose their sight, sometimes they learn to use their other senses better than before." I think this is an amazing child's view of faith. When we walk by faith and not sight, we can hold onto the promise that God has given us even in the midst of chaos.

If it is possible to impart gifts to you via a book, then I want to do it.
Let me pray over you: "What I have I give to you, freely as I have received, freely I give." I pray that you would be filled with the Spirit. I pray that the Lord would give you the gift of prophecy and all the gifts of the Spirit.

What is God saying to your heart?

_____

_____

_____

_____

_____

_____

_____

_____

_____

_____

_____

_____

_____

_____

_____

_____

_____

Chapter 11

Now Is The Time To Love The Unlovely

"If I speak with the tongues of men and of angels, but do not have love, I have become a noisy gong or a clanging cymbal. If I have the gift of prophecy, and know all mysteries and all knowledge; and if I have all faith, so as to remove mountains, but do not have love, I am nothing. If I have the gift of prophecy and can fathom all mysteries and all knowledge, and if I have a faith that can move mountains, but do not have love, I am nothing."   1 Corinthians 13: 1-3

God is love. If we speak in the tongues of men and of angels but don't have God's love, we have nothing. I hear so many people say that if Christians went around loving people in the world, we would live in an amazing place. I believe this is true. Jesus did a great job of loving the unlovely. In this new move of God, He is calling all the outcasts and prodigals to Him. If we want to join in on what God is doing, we will need to love the unlovely just like Jesus did.

Loving people does not always include witnessing to them. Not all people are ready to be witnessed to. We need to ask the Holy Spirit where they are in their walk with Him and love them wherever they are. The Holy Spirit will guide us if He wants us to tell them about Christ. Sometimes people just need to know we care about them. We can plant seeds so that God can mature them in the future. Just like a prophetic word needs to be in God's timing, witnessing needs to be in step with God's timing as well. Witnessing to someone out of God's timing or in a forceful way may harm them more than it will help them. We can witness to someone when the Holy Spirit tells us to or when we feel they are ready. When the timing is right, God can move powerfully! Witnessing needs to always be done with a heart of love, not the need to earn a spiritual badge.

One of the most amazing lessons the Lord taught me was to love my neighbor. I was praying one time and God told me to "love my neighbor." He reminded me of an old neighbor who lived in a former neighborhood that I lived in. My neighbor was often drunk. He had a drunken fight on our front porch one time. He knocked on our door at 2 am and asked us to call the police. He was someone that most people may have referred to as unlovely. Later that day, my son's soccer practice was moved to an alternate location right near my old neighbor's back yard. I prayed, "God, if you want me to say hi, could you have him come outside?" I looked over, and my old neighbor walked outside to grill burgers on his back porch. This gave me the faith I needed, and I knew God wanted me to talk to my neighbor. I went over and chatted with him for a while. He shared many deep stories of how he had been wounded by the church. When my son was done with his soccer practice, he came over. We talked until we had to leave. We really felt like we needed to spend more time with him, but we had to go somewhere at that time.

We were elated when God showed us that my son had "accidently" left his shin guards at his house, and we had to stop by his house and get them. We stopped by the next day before my son's soccer game. At this point, we felt God prompting us to pray with him and his wife. We asked him if we could pray with him, and he said yes. He mentioned that his dad drank, and drinking was in his family line. We prayed for deliverance from things hindering him from his family line and that God would touch him. We saw him a few months later at a neighborhood yard sale. He said that a pastor had been talking with him and he was going to visit a local church down the street that Sunday. His wife said, "Wow, prayer is powerful."

There are many times that I have asked God to show me who He wants me to be friends with. Some of the friends that he leads me to are never who I would expect. He often paired me up with someone who was broken and someone who the church may call unlovely. In the Bible, Jesus was always looked down on by religious leaders for who He hung out with. Jesus loves sinners. Do you hang out with unlovely people? How about normal people or weird people? Jesus was the first to hang out with a woman when His culture said not to. Do you hang out with anyone that our church culture says not to hang out with? Somewhere we have gotten the idea that we are not supposed to hang out with sinners. We don't have to do things with them that we are convicted that we should not do, but we should hang out with them and love them. We should have a healthy amount of friends in our lives who believe other things. If not, we are being exclusive and putting ourselves in a bubble.

We also need to be careful of offense. When we get offended about everything we see and hear, it blocks us from loving others. Don't get offended if someone uses different words than you. Someone may use the word lucky. You use the word blessed. Don't get offended. Just realize that they use a different word.

I know God has healed me of a religious mindset. I believe that most Christians have some aspect of a religious mindset that is not of God. This mindset may have an exclusive feeling to be holy, but in reality it is holier-than-thou. God is doing amazing things with all types of denominations and people groups. He is not exclusive to one group. If you feel that He is or that your denomination is better than others, you may be struggling with a religious mindset. You can always pray that God will heal your heart and set you free. Do you have a Christ-like mindset or a religious mindset?

I believe God is going to use people in this upcoming revival who love the unlovely. He is calling in the people that are called "outcasts." He is calling those who may even have been wounded by the church.

A pastor who loves sinners may not preach exactly the same style as other pastors do. Maybe he loves the unlovely and would rather do what God wants him to do than what people feel he should do. What about you? Think of someone in your town who others may feel is unlovely. Think of a way that you could love them today, and write it down. Make an attempt to show that you care for them the next time you see them.

What is God saying to your heart?

_____
_____
_____
_____
_____
_____
_____
_____
_____
_____
_____
_____
_____
_____
_____

Chapter 12

Now Is The Time to Share Your Testimony

"For the testimony of Jesus is the spirit of prophecy."
Revelation 19:10b (NKJ)

Revelation 19:10 is one of the most powerful verses I know. It means that the testimony of what Jesus has done in your life can be used to set other people free. This is the spirit of prophecy. This means that God can take all the hard times you've had and all the tough seasons that you went through and use them to help others. The enemy may have overplayed his hand during a hard season of your life, but God can use it for good. Sharing your testimony can help someone else be set free from the snares of the enemy.

By sharing your testimony, you will allow God to speak truth into others' lives. The truth that you share can replace lies or strongholds in someone else's life. Deliverance is replacing truth for a lie. I have had many lies replaced with truth in my life, and I find great joy every time I am set free from the bondage of a lie. You may be called to share your testimony only with other people one-on-one. You may be called to share it with the public. God will guide you on what you should do. If your testimony is painful, it might be something just for you to help people one-on-one when the time arises. When I hear a prophetic person speak, I can feel God break things off of me spiritually. This is so cool. In the past, I have wondered why a speaker was rambling about things that happened to him. God showed me that through our stories, He is moving mountains and setting people free. Our stories can help others receive truth in their lives.

My wilderness season was sealed by the Lord. I do not usually share specific details of it with anyone unless God specifically asks me to. This is because I have been healed of the more painful parts. I don't want to dredge them out again and again. If God has healed you in some area, it might be healthier to move on and not look back. In this instance, you would not want to share your testimony, unless God asks you to share it.

Angie Smith lost an infant after child birth. Their baby had a rare birth defect, and they knew that she would not live very long. She started a website with the baby's name, Audrey Caroline. She was able to share her story with many moms, and her testimony was very powerful. This is the spirit of prophecy at work. God also gave my friend Susan Noviello a very powerful testimony.

Susan shares, "By the age of 29 all the pain and dysfunction of my life caught up with me. I never sought emotional healing from my parent's tumultuous divorce and the abandonment from each of my family members left me living on my own by the age of 17. Recently divorced myself and without a job, suicide appeared to be a viable option. I turned to New Age for answers. However, the more I studied, the more confused I became. New Age takes many teachings from different spiritual disciplines. I knew they couldn't all be true. In search for some answers, I took the tools I learned from New Age and began to meditate. My focus became to seek for the absolute truth. My meditations began in small increments, and then I began increasing the length of my sessions each day. I became consumed with wanting to know the absolute truth. The more I meditated, the easier it was for me to enter and focus. My meditations increased to 2 - 4 hours with no loss of focus. At this time, I was seeking for what the truth was. Then one day, I entered into a mediation and I saw a bright light. I stayed focused on the light and Jesus appeared to me in a vision. He told me that He was the way, the truth, and the life. I had the answer I was looking for; however, I did not find joy or relief in the answer. I was honestly very angry that the truth was Jesus. New Age allows for autonomy and control in one's own life. My view of Christianity was skewed. I saw the God of Christianity as one who had a lot of rules that must be obeyed and I had no desire to go to church with Christians who I felt acted elitist. After a two-week wrestle with God I chose to turn my life over to

Jesus and receive the life that was available to me through the shedding of Jesus's blood on the cross. I searched and found that some Christians did have a lot of freedom and happiness. Some were very giving and humble and not elitist at all. These were the Christians who were truly like Christ."

Susan is an amazing friend. Since Susan had this experience, she can now relate to New Age people, and has a powerful prophetic ministry just by being available to touch people that God brings across her path.

Testimonies of what Jesus is doing can ignite a fire in you. They are so exciting because they are God stories. They are God's way of teaching others. There is nothing more wonderful than something God is doing. Write down a testimony of something God has done in your life. You can write about when you became a believer and any trials that you have overcome. Will a story that you have written encourage someone? If God is leading you, share it with someone that it may encourage.

_____

_____

_____

_____

_____

_____

_____

_____

Chapter 13

Now is the Time to Realize God's Power is Perfect in Our Weakness

But he said to me, "My grace is sufficient for you, for my power is made perfect in weakness." Therefore, I will boast all the more gladly about my weaknesses, so that Christ's power may rest on me.
2 Corinthians 12:9

My friend Brandie asked me to go to a Beth Moore conference to celebrate our birthdays. It was at this conference that God commissioned me to write this book. He commissioned Brandie to write one as well. Before this conference, I thought I could not write a book, but God revealed to me there that I was being extremely selfish. He said that if He wanted to write a book through me, then I should realize that I could do it in His strength. His strength is made perfect in my weakness. I accepted the assignment from the Lord to write the book and decided to have the faith that He would show up to help me write it.

The realization that God's strength is made perfect in our weakness is a strategy to solve almost any problem in our lives where we are having trouble. I think one of the biggest issues right now in our world is being distracted. There are smart phones, tv shows, movies and the Internet all providing entertainment available 24 hours a day, and they are vying for our time. I know that I go through seasons where busyness and distraction prevent me from spending time with the Lord. In our day and age, it is very discouraging to deal with these issues.

God showed me a solution. By identifying my weaknesses, I am on the road to allowing God's power to prove Himself strong. We can ask God to help us spend time with Him in the midst of this generation of distraction. He can remind us to spend time with Him and help us keep a good balance from being too distracted. By trusting Him in this, we are set free from guilt and shame. He can help us with gentle reminders. He has also taught me to set aside a special time with Him each day. Even if I am busy with my children and I only have a limited amount of time to spare, spending time with God will remind me that He is my first love. Jesus said, "I am the vine; you are the branches. If you remain in me and I in you, you will bear much fruit; apart from me you can do nothing" (John 15:5). If you allow intimacy with God to be your top priority, you can walk in step with the Holy Spirit. If your relationship with God is not your top priority, do not expect to walk in step with the Holy Spirit. The enemy often tries to distract us from spending time with God.

God also gave me strategies for busyness and distraction. Sometimes I need to slow down and rest. I can't hear from God if I don't take time to rest. We will examine what it means to truly rest in Christ the next chapter.

As a mom and friend to others, I need to answer texts and encourage others, but I don't want to be so overwhelmed with them that I can't function. I also don't want to just give up my iPhone. I can pray and ask God to keep me in balance. Balance is the key. I know a few people that are just really likable people. Congenial people are wonderful, but they need to beware that not everyone can have thirty close friends. That would be a lot of texts to reply to. I had a friend who knew that she did not have time to be my friend, so she prayed that I would find another friend. God put me in touch with an amazing lady that I just love. At first I felt a little rejected, but then I realized that the first person home schooled her children and she probably did not have time for another friend. If you are constantly busy and stressed out, you may need to uproot some things in your life that you do not have time for. When we pray in faith, believing that God wants to help us not to be distracted and He guides us to rest and think of Him throughout our day, we pray in His will. We are believing He will do it, and He hears our prayers.

You may be struggling with something right now. Tell the Lord what you are struggling with. He already knows what it is, but He longs for you to be honest and tell Him. Now is the time to pray and ask God to take your weakness and make His power strong in this area of your life. This will be one of those special God powered areas because you know that you cannot do it in your own strength, so you can easily give Him full credit. God uses the power of the weak to shame the wise (1 Corinthians 1:27).

What is God saying to your heart?

_____

_____

_____

_____

_____

_____

_____

_____

_____

_____

_____

_____

_____

_____

Chapter 14

Now Is The Time for Rest and Restoration

Therefore, since the promise of entering his rest still stands, let us be careful that none of you be found to have fallen short of it.
Hebrews 4:1

A huge key to contentment when walking in the Spirit is to master the art of resting. When we learn to rest in the Lord, He can restore us. It's exciting to walk in the supernatural things of God, but if we don't learn to enter into God's rest, we can lack contentment. God commands us to rest (Exodus 20: 8-10). Resting is a beautiful thing, and it is a key to being content when things are not supernatural at the moment. I've also learned that rest is a great thing because if I am resting, then that means I am letting God fight my battles for me. Jesus said, "Come to me, all you who are weary and burdened, and I will give you rest. Take my yoke upon you and learn from me, for I am gentle and humble in heart, and you will find rest for your souls. For my yoke is easy and my burden is light" (Matthew 11:28-30).

When we are resting in Christ, we trust in Him.

This means we are not worrying or trying to fight our battles on our own. We can actually rest and let Jesus fight for us. Are you constantly struggling with fighting your own battles? Learning the art of resting in the Lord can make a great change in our lives. Jesus says that "His yoke is easy and His burden is light." If we learn to rest in Christ, we will find that He carries our load for us. His finished work sustains us. When we learn to rest in our identity in Christ, it can change our lives.

I went through a rough season of warfare during my wilderness season. I realized that I was not trusting Jesus with my warfare. I would give it to Him until something new came up, and then I would take it back and try to solve the problem on my own. It was when I realized that God was bigger than my biggest problem, that I began to rest in Him. I can pray and tell Him what is going on, and then hand over my problem to Him. I sure wasn't going to be able to fix it in my own strength. If I begin to worry, it is a warning sign that I've begun to take my problem back in my own hands. Do you have something that you are struggling with? Know that God is bigger than your biggest problem!

I realized that if I began to talk or "gossip" about my problem with my friends, it was the equivalent of taking my problem back into my own hands. This was actually poison to me. I realized that if I really needed to talk about something, I first should talk about my problem to God. Then, if I still needed to discuss it, I could talk with a counselor or a mentor. Some people in the Christian community view seeking a counselor as negative, but that is opposite of the truth. When we see a counselor, we are actually taking a very positive step towards healing. When we are willing to admit we need help and seek a counselor, we reveal that we care very much about those we love. We are willing to get help. The Holy Spirit is our counselor and He is great to seek first, but God uses people, such as Christian counselors and mentors, to help us as well.

When we take time out to rest and spend time with God, He refills us and restores us. I think it's interesting how often the Bible mentions that Jesus and the disciples went to a quiet place and rested.

> Then, because so many people were coming and going that they did not even have a chance to eat, He said to them, "Come with me by yourselves to a quiet place and get some rest." Mark 6:31

When we have so much going on and we are pouring into others, we have to take time to rest and get refilled. In a professional car race, the race car drivers take pit stops during the race. They get refueled, and they get their tires changed. A car can be symbolic of ministry. We need to make sure we stop and rest and get refueled in our ministries. Tires are also symbolic of the Holy Spirit. We need to make sure our tires are filled up so that we can keep running the race set before us! We need to make sure we are filled with the Holy Spirit!

I have realized that I need to plan strategic times of rest in my day. I need to take these "pit stops" and get refilled. These don't just happen automatically. If you don't usually stop to rest in your day, take a step back and look at your daily routine. See if you can find out why you don't stop to rest. A friend once told me that he never rested. He said that he was taught as a child that if he rested and had down time, that it would allow the enemy to have time to put wrong thoughts in his mind. Because of this lie, my friend never rested. The enemy is going to put wrong thoughts in our minds. We have to cast them down, but this is not a good reason to avoid rest. This person needed healing from a fear of resting. Can you see how the enemy worked a lie into his heart so that he almost never refueled in the Lord? The enemy may also tell us that resting is lazy but it is not. Thankfully the Lord can set us free from any lies so we can learn to rest in Him.

When I think of practicing the presence of God, I think of entering into God's rest. Entering God's rest starts with obedience.

Therefore, since the promise of entering his rest still stands, let us be careful that none of you be found to have fallen short of it. For we also have had the good news proclaimed to us, just as they did; but the message they heard was of no value to them, because they did not share the faith of those who obeyed. Now we who have believed enter that rest, just as God has said, "So I declared on oath in my anger, 'They shall never enter my rest.'" And yet his works have been finished since the creation of the world. For somewhere he has spoken about the seventh day in these words: "On the seventh day God rested from all his works." And again in the passage above he says, "They shall never enter my rest." Therefore, since it still remains for some to enter that rest, and since those who formerly had the good news proclaimed to them did not go in because of their disobedience, God again set a certain day, calling it "Today." This he did when a long time later he spoke through David, as in the passage already quoted: "Today, if you hear his voice, do not harden your hearts." For if Joshua had given them rest, God would not have spoken later about another day. There remains, then, a Sabbath-rest for the people of God; for anyone who enters God's rest also rests from their works, just as God did from his. Let us, therefore, make every effort to enter that rest, so that no one will perish by following their example of disobedience.　　　Hebrews 4:1-11

When you hear God's voice, do not harden your heart to what He is asking you to do. He will give you the strength to do it. When we enter into God's rest, we can feel His Presence in the state of peace. God does not force us to obey Him, He gives us a choice. If we choose not to obey, we will not feel God's peace and we will not rest in Him. God is patient. He lovingly helps us when we confess our sin, and He turns us back to the right path of obedience. He will even teach us valuable lessons through our mistakes.

　　　When we worry about something, we are really praying every negative thing we can imagine about it. The opposite of worry is faith. What if we imagined every good thing we could about a situation? Some positive thinking non Christians may have stumbled upon the Biblical principal of faith. They may be following God's principles better than some Christians. When we use these principles and include the Lord, it is powerful. When we imagine the best and give our problems to the Lord as they come up, God's peace guards our hearts and minds.

> Do not be anxious about anything, but in every situation, by prayer and petition, with thanksgiving, present your requests to God. And the peace of God, which transcends all understanding, will guard your hearts and your minds in Christ Jesus. Philippians 4:6-7

We can tell Him that we are thankful that He is going to take care of the issue, and put it in His hands. He may ask us to take steps towards the solution, but other than that, we can wait in peace.

Jesus is the Prince of Peace. If we rest in Him, we will feel His peace. Thinking about resting in Him throughout the day helps me focus on Him and talk to Him. It also helps me stay positive and content. It keeps me from wondering who I am in Christ. It keeps me from worry when I have not heard God's voice in a while. It helps me draw from His completed work when I constantly live in a state of rest. I am resting in my identity in Christ when I have totally surrendered and am trusting in what Christ is doing in my life. The Lord replied, "My Presence will go with you, and I will give you rest" (Exodus 33:14). When we are in a state of rest we can often feel God's Presence.

There are a few things the Bible says can hinder us from entering into God's rest. Fear keeps us from entering into God's rest (Psalms 95:10-11). Fear is a lack of trust in God. When we don't trust God, we don't believe that He will meet our needs. We believe we have to solve our problems ourselves. When we fear, we need to fix things ourselves and be in control. I will talk more about how to ask God to heal you of fear in the next chapter.

God also showed me that sometimes we try to escape from issues in our lives rather than deal with them. Escape can be an unhealthy form of rest. It is good to escape when we take a vacation, but it is not good to escape the issues in our lives that we need to deal with. Escape can easily become a bad habit. Video games or the Internet can be a form of escape from the realities of life. We may need to pray for healing. Living in the moment in a state of rest in our identity in Christ is something we have to practice. It doesn't just automatically happen when we become a Christian.

Jesus said, "I am the vine; you are the branches. If you remain in me and I in you, you will bear much fruit; apart from me you can do nothing" (John 15:5). Resting in the Lord reminds me of staying in the vine. I am finding rest in God's constant Presence. When it is time to love someone and minister to someone, I am rested and ready. I can stay calm and be in a state of rest as I minister and draw from God's wisdom and power.

There are many times in my life when I get busy, and I forget to rest. I am still learning to master the art of resting in the Lord. I have learned that fasting something once a week can really help me learn to refocus. Fasting is a powerful tool that can help us in the area of resting. If we fast something, we are taking a break from doing it. This is the same concept as resting. This is the same concept as taking a Sabbath rest from work on Sunday. I started a new thing this year where I try to fast my iPhone and talk to the Lord while I wait in the carpool line to pick my children up from school. The Lord has honored this greatly, and I have been very surprised to learn that He really blesses fasting. It brings breakthrough, healing, and intimacy with the Lord. God also loves it when His children are not legalistic about fasting. If I need to get on my phone to answer a call or send out an email during a carpool pick up, I know that it is okay for me to do these things. I don't want to be legalistic and not be free to do things in my life when I need to do them.

Do you stop to rest in your daily life? What are some ways that you rest? This is a very important discipline in our lives. Learning to rest in Christ will give you great freedom and peace in Christ.

Pray with me:
Lord, teach us how to rest in our identity in You. Help us to give you our burdens right now. You are bigger than all of our biggest problems. Nothing is impossible for you. Help us to let go, trust you, and find rest for our souls.

Chapter 15

Now Is The Time To Overcome Fear

"There is no fear in love, but perfect love casts out fear. For fear has to do with punishment, and whoever fears has not been perfected in love."
1 John 4:18 (NKJV)

Fear is rampant in America. Everyone seems to be afraid. There was a season when our children were very young and our family decided to go a few years without a TV. During this time, my husband and I went on a trip, stayed at a hotel, and watched a segment of the news. I noticed the news stories had fearful themes behind them. We went to sleep, and I ended up having two nightmares about the stories that I saw on the news that night. It was then that I realized how much fear the media places in the minds of viewers through the news. If you don't want to be fearful, you might want to turn off the news. You can always check what's going on in our world online as an alternative.

A lot of people fear the government and who will

be elected as president. The truth is, if we put our trust in God, we don't have anything to fear. God is in control of our world, not the government. God puts leaders in their place. Sometimes He gives America what we are asking for, even if it's not what He wants and sometimes He puts someone in place that He can use for His glory. No matter who wins the elections, God is in control. We are blessed to even have an election. Not every country has elections. I pray we always have elections in America.

The enemy is also instilling fear of the end times. To me the end times means that Satan is furious because his time is short. By that definition, I know we are in the end times. Satan is definitely furious that his time is short. However, we are Christians. God gave us all the tools and blessing we need to thrive right now. If we can accelerate in the church and grab a hold of these tools, there is no reason to be afraid. In fact, these tools will help us rise up with courage! It's important as Christians to stay positive. We need to be rooted in Christ by knowing who we are in Christ. We need to constantly talk about how we can thrive spiritually because we are God's children. God has not given us a spirit of fear but of power, love, and a sound mind (2 Timothy 1:7).

I went to a ladies retreat in Connecticut where the leaders prayed that we would be healed of all of our fears. After the retreat, God spent over a year showing me my fears. He healed me of fears I didn't even know that I had. Fear is not from God, so we know that it's from the enemy. You can pray that God will heal you of all fear.

Some churches have a fear of the supernatural. If we want to be strong in the last days, we are going to have to break through the fear of the supernatural and realize God does miracles and many things that we cannot explain with our rational minds. We can look in the Bible and see all kinds of supernatural experiences. God intended for us to have "supernatural experiences" with Him. Somewhere along the way, some Christians became afraid that we would just seek after experiences instead of God, so they declared all supernatural experiences as bad. We have to change this mindset because God is a supernatural God. Being in an intimate relationship with Him includes having supernatural experiences. There comes a point where these experiences become normal for someone who is close to God. We shouldn't be afraid of them. The enemy would love for us to have a stronghold of fear of God's supernatural power.

There are other terms that cause fear in Christians. Specific words pull up fear. One of them is the word revelation. This means hearing from God. It is important to hear from God. Some people fear the word deliverance. Deliverance is from God and is basically replacing lies with truth. It can also include rebuking Satan or telling him to "Be Gone!" When I do this, I try to make sure I replace it with the Holy Spirit.

Matthew 10: 7-8 (NKJV) says, "And as you go, preach, saying, 'The kingdom of heaven is at hand.'

Heal the sick, raise the dead, cleanse the lepers, cast out demons. Freely you received, freely give." If we are afraid, God is gracious to help us overcome our fears. When we get to a point where God uses us to heal the sick, raise the dead, cleanse the lepers, and cast out demons, then we will have revival all the time. This is what God intended to be a part of the normal Christian life.

Another word I feel people fear is when someone says the word happiness in the Church. The Bible says, "I seek my happiness in the Lord, and He gives me my heart's desire. I give myself to the Lord; trust in Him, and He helps me. He makes my righteousness shine like the noonday sun" (Psalm 37:4-6). Another good verse about happiness is Matthew 25:21: "His master replied, 'Well done, good and faithful servant! You have been faithful with a few things; I will put you in charge of many things. Come and share your master's happiness.'" You are obviously not going to be happy all the time, but please know that God wants His children to be happy. God is a good father.

We have to be careful that the enemy does not give us a poverty mindset. You may notice you have a poverty mindset if you complain often, and you think God wants you to suffer all of your life. There is a certain amount of suffering in the world, but if you have food and you are not thrown into prison for your faith, rejoice! You don't have it so bad. God longs for his children to have revelation, deliverance, joy, and happiness in their lives.

In America we have spiritual poverty. We may have material blessings but these can't meet our deepest need like God can. If you look at Hollywood, you can see people trying to put money and fame in the place of their need for God. The result is usually someone famous checking into rehab. Material things cannot meet our deepest needs. Only God can. We may have storms that bring harder financial times, but it will be even more amazing in the fact that we will be spiritually nourished. Do not fear. God has not given us a spirit of fear. God has a great plan. In the midst of hard times, God's light will shine even brighter. It's an amazing time to be a part of God's work! He's going to bless His people beyond their imagination. Those that are not ready for these things may be caught off guard. Some who are not ready, may want to give up after hard times. Never give up! Know that God will uphold us with his righteous right hand (Isaiah 14:10).

Let us not become weary in doing good, for at the proper time we will reap a harvest if we do not give up. Galatians 6:9

Do you struggle with fear? Would you believe me if I told you that God wants to heal you of every single one of your fears? Fear is not from God, and the Lord longs to set you free! Spend some time with the Lord and tell Him your fears. Ask Him to set you free.

Chapter 16

Now is the Time To Unite in Love

"Finally, all of you, be like-minded, be sympathetic, love one another, be compassionate and humble."
1 Peter 3:8

If you have children, you may get frustrated when your children fight. I know that I do. Can you imagine how God must feel to see His children fighting? If you look on Facebook, you can see one ministry attacking another ministry, this ministry calling that one false. God longs for His children to unite. That means that we should pray for other ministries instead of publicly or privately bashing them. The enemy knows that he can hurt the Church if he can cause division. He knows that "a divided house cannot stand" (Mark 3:25).

We need to be responsible for who we speak evil about. The Bible says this is poison. James 3:8-11 says, "But no human being can tame the tongue. It is a restless evil, full of deadly poison. With the tongue we praise our Lord and Father, and with it we curse human beings, who have been made in God's likeness. Out of the same mouth come praise and cursing. My brothers and sisters, this should not be. Can both fresh water and salt water flow from the same spring?" Sometimes if I'm praying and I can't get a breakthrough, I will pray "Lord, forgive me if I've cursed anyone with my tongue." This prayer is powerful, and sometimes I can instantly hear from the Lord. Cursing someone with our tongue can be a roadblock to our intimacy with the Lord. Some of my friends feel that they are just "warning" people that other people are false. If the Lord did not specifically ask you to warn someone that someone else is false, do not do it. You may be bashing the bride.

One of my friends received a picture from the Lord of Jesus's body being hit by a hammer. She was reading the book *Exposing The Accuser of The Brethren* by Francis Frangipane. The Lord told her that the picture meant that some Christians were bashing Christ's body. The Lord showed her that she was doing this. She says that she was "beating the body of Christ by criticizing and judging them." She felt that she was being harsh and critical instead of being gentle, patient, loving, and kind. She learned that kindness starts with loving our family members first, and then it extends to the worldwide body of Christ. "For when they see a need, instead of becoming critical, they cast down the accuser of the brethren and they pray" (Francis Frangipane).

God has revealed to me that the key to the Christian life is to love. God says, "Love the Lord your

God will all your heart, soul, mind, and strength and love your neighbor as yourself" (Luke 10:27). These are the two key commands to the purpose of life. If we speak in the tongues of men and of angels but we don't have love, we have nothing.

Many Christians spend a lot of time defending their doctrine. This is a huge distraction from loving others. I love this quote from Reinard Bonnke: "The Bible says we are to be God's witnesses not His lawyers." We somehow have gotten distracted from our main goal as a Christian. God has placed in my heart an uneasiness when I see Christians bashing other Christians.

I went to a Baptist university. While I was there, some students told me that I should not go to the church next door because they preached "the prosperity gospel." I wondered what this meant. Years later, I noticed that some of my friends on Facebook regularly bashed another pastor with similar beliefs. I prayed for the Lord to reveal His heart to me concerning this topic. God showed me Luke 6:22. It says, "Blessed are you when people hate you, when they exclude you and insult you and reject your name as evil, because of the Son of Man." God was showing me that He backed the pastor my friends were attacking, and that this pastor receives a blessing every time someone speaks evil about him. There were positive biblical principles to overcome the enemy that one group of people understood and another group of people did not understand. Since one group did not understand the principles, they labeled groups of people who believe the Bible and the positive principals as false. They coined this term as the prosperity gospel, yet the wrong pastors are being labeled with this term. This has spread all across this denomination and a few others. Let me tell you, this is not from God. Another church may be different than your church, but that does not mean that God is not moving powerfully there.

God wants you to overcome the wilderness, not stay in it forever. That does not mean that you will be rich or famous. Most of the pastors who preach the positive principal that God wants to bless you and get you out of the wilderness, do not preach that God will give you money or wealth if you follow Him. They preach that you need to be positive to overcome the wilderness. Yet, positive pastors are labeled this often, even if it is not what they preach. Most of the people who do the bashing have never visited these churches for themselves, but they base their facts on what other people say. If you do not understand someone else's ministry, ask God before you decide to take a public stand that they are false. I believe the term prosperity gospel has caused many Christians to have deep pride towards the way they think and publicly act towards other ministries. If you have publicly bashed a group for this, you might want to confess it before God and pray to seek His heart towards other ministries. If you do think that a church is teaching something incorrectly, pray for them.

I have been in complete shock since the Lord

has shown me that the people who cause the most division in the church are Christians who bash other Christians. We are called to love our brothers and sisters, have mercy on them, and pray for them.

You don't have to be a minister to have a ministry. God has called everyone to the ministry of love. Some people I know who love God the most are people who are not pastors, but they were people who understood that their job was a ministry to love those in their workplace.

I was invited to a home church one time. The leader ran a MOPS group, and she invited me to check it out. I went for a few weeks, and then the Lord showed me that the home church was a cult. They were saved, but they had major doctrinal issues. They believed that you could not use medicine if you were sick. After I left the church, I was able to set up a time to pray with the mom that invited me. The night before we prayed together, the Lord woke me up in the middle of the night and asked me not to tell her that her church was a cult. He told me that He wanted to tell her Himself. Since her dad was the leader of this group, I believe she would not have been able to receive this information from me. She needed to hear it from God Himself. Was this group saved? Yes, I believe they were; however, because of a few lies they believed instead of the truth, they were not walking in the freedom that God gives His children. The Word says we are all being renewed day by day (2 Corinthians 4:16). I have my own share of lies that are being replaced with truth. It does not in help this ministry if I bash them and call them false. The best thing I can do for them is to pray and seek God's heart for them.

What is God saying to your heart?

_____

_____

_____

_____

_____

_____

_____

_____

_____

_____

_____

_____

_____

_____

_____

_____

_____

_____

_____

_____

Chapter 17

Now Is The Time To Pray In Faith

"Now faith is the substance of things hoped for, the evidence of things not seen." Hebrews 11:1 (NKJV)

The Lord told me that Super Bowl 50 was prophetic of revival in America. He showed me many levels of how the Charlotte Panthers were part of this. First the Panthers lost the game, and this revival is to call in the ones people tend to call "losers" or outcasts. Even if the world sees them that way, God does not. God sees them as beautiful. Another thing He showed me was how the Panthers were known for giving the football to kids after they scored. He said that those who are a part of this revival will be comfortable passing the ball to children and everyone will need to have faith like a child. When missionary Heidi Baker prays for blind people to see, the first group of people she calls to come help her are children. She will tell you that she calls them down because they have great faith. There is no better way to see God move than to believe that He can do it and He will do it. We can get in a faith-filled mindset by having faith like a child.

Faith comes by hearing and hearing by the word of God. I went to a conference with an awesome cowboy missionary, David Hogan. I'll never forget when he prayed over me. He prayed three words: "Bless you baby." I had been through a very traumatic experience in my wilderness season, and these three words led me back to my chair where I sobbed like a baby for about 30 minutes. In this time, God healed me from the inside out. David Hogan taught us that we have to have "Now Faith." Not later in heaven faith, "Now Faith." David Hogan also has his grandkids stand and pray over people when he prays for them. Eventually, they begin to whisper things in his ear that God tells them, and he then calls those people up for prayer. If you are preaching or praying for someone, call your children up to minister with you. They will not only model what you are doing, but their faith may move mountains. This could seriously change the stigma of being a pastor's child, if a pastor proves to his children that they are just as important to him as his ministry, by having them serve with him.

Having faith is very important. Some pastors are afraid to discuss this topic, but it is in the Bible. The Bible says many times that someone's faith made them well. They either prayed in faith believing that God would answer their prayer, or someone else's faith opened a door for God to heal them. We need to be a generation of now faith. My faith can't heal anyone, only

God can heal, but my faith can open a door to allow God to heal someone, so it is very important. One of the first examples of faith was Mary, the mother of Jesus. She asked Jesus to turn water into wine. He told her that it was not yet time. I believe that she looked in His eyes with a look that said, "I believe that you can do this." She told the people to do whatever Jesus told them to do. Jesus then looked to the father, and I believe His heart was turned. Mary had so much faith that her son could do it that God said, "Let's turn some water into wine. This sounds like a great first miracle."

Stretching your faith muscle can be painful. Sometimes you will need to hold onto a promise the Lord gave you even if you are the only person to believe it. An angel said to Mary, "Blessed is she who has believed that the Lord would fulfill his promises to her!" (Luke 1:45). I had times where the Lord would speak a promise to me and everyone around me would give me a bad report. They said, "Oh, that won't happen. You are not supposed to do that." I had to lean on my promise from God and His promise alone. Each time, God did what He said He would do, and it was amazing! I have had a few times where even my closest friends and family did not support me. I learned to lean solely on God during those times.

I have also learned to say no when God asks me to say no. This is not an easy thing to do when other people want me to say yes. I've learned that saying yes to someone, when God is asking me to say no, can bring me years of heartache. I have learned that it is a lot easier to say no when God asks me to, than to go into a wilderness season. The Lord is also faithful to get us out of a mess if we have made a mistake.

There was a time when God told me that we were in the end times (which means Satan is furious because his time is short) and I needed to pray in faith if I wanted to defeat the enemy. Praying in faith is something that God showed me I had to do. I remember a time when I used to pray to God and say, "God please heal this person and I believe that you will." One day we were praying for someone and Kevin, one of my mentors from Kainos in East Hampton, Connecticut, came up to me and said, "God said to tell you 'I will.'" It blew me away, and it meant so much to me because I often pray "I believe that you will" when I pray to God. He was answering me by saying, "I will." God was showing me that having faith is a very important part of prayer. James 1:6 says to pray in faith and do not doubt because if we doubt we are "like a wave of the sea that is blown and tossed by the wind."

We can also use our spiritual authority in Christ and command sickness to leave someone in Jesus name. I have seen sickness leave people when I have done this. When doing this, replace sickness with health and wholeness and the Holy Spirit. The Lord will guide you on how to pray for someone.

Have you ever thought about praying in faith? Do you think you could pray a prayer and not believe God will do it? If your prayer is in line with God's will, the Bible says God will answer your prayer if you pray in faith, believing that He will do it.

Chapter 18

Now Is The Time For Revival

"The harvest is plentiful but the workers are few. Ask the Lord of the harvest, therefore, to send out workers into his harvest field."
Luke 10:2

    I believe that the Presence of God is going to be so powerful in the coming days, that we will want nothing more than to worship in spirit and in truth. Those who enter into God's Presence will radiate like Moses did (Exodus 34:30). We will have so much light and joy that we will stand out among the darkness. The Lord spoke to me one time and told me that He was going to "take the shine out of the stars in the sky and place it on His intercessors." He showed me Daniel 12:3. It says, "Those who are wise will shine like the brightness of the heavens, and those who lead many to righteousness, like the stars for ever and ever." God is showing me that we will radiate with God's light and joy after we spend time in His Presence (Psalm 16:11).

    This book was written to accelerate you so God can use you for revival. Now is the time to seek the Lord for what He wants you to do in this revival. In 2007, Julie Meyer, former International House of Prayer worship leader, had a dream that angels were lining up for revival and the Lord said, "Now is not yet the time." She recently had a dream to pray for the revival because God was ready. He is said, "Now is the time." Psalms 104:4 reveals, "He sends his angels like the winds, his servants like flames of fire" (NLT). Expect angels to be a part of this revival. Julie saw them lining up to help us, and the Bible says they are sent by God to do His work.

A friend of mine has a young daughter named Althea. She had a prophetic dream about revival. God also used her dream to confirm this book. She saw a yellow ring, and God said it was symbolic of all the people who believed in God. She saw lightning coming out of the yellow ring. God said the lightning was symbolic of all the people who were going to tell other people about God, and the Lord said, "It is now. It is time."

When I originally had the encounter where the angel gave me the message, "Now is the Time," I started singing, "Now, now is the time to worship." The Lord showed me that He is going to bring us into a new level of worship. I believe that people will freely worship God like never before.

This book is a tool to equip all denominations to be filled with the Holy Spirit and pray prophetically. To be a part of revival, we will need to hear the voice of God, and a key to hearing His revelation is being filled with the Holy Spirit. We will need to do what we see the Father doing, just as Jesus did. Then we need the Holy

Spirit's power to do it.

The Lord had me go to Great Wolf Lodge with my kids and my friend Brandie.
On December 24, 2005 at 5 am the Lord told us,

"There is a shift in the atmosphere. The angels are here. I am releasing my prophetic army. I am starting a fire. You will see miracles like never before. Prepare the church nurseries. (This is symbolic because churches will be overflowing with new believers and they will need discipleship.) You will see salvation, healing, and deliverance. The new believers will look messy, but do not discard them. Prophetic prayer and humility are the keys to bearing fruit in this revival. Now is The Time!"

The Lord also said that the revival will come in waves. My son, who was 9 at the time, was awakened the same night, and he saw a crystal like a pure bride and he saw the disciples near a fire which we felt meant this revival will be similar to the book of Acts. The crystal is also symbolic for discernment. Many in the revival will have discernment and be able to "see through" others' heart motives and pray for them.

"And afterward,
I will pour out my Spirit on all people.
Your sons and daughters will prophesy,
your old men will dream dreams,
your young men will see visions.

Even on my servants, both men and women,
I will pour out my Spirit in those days.
I will show wonders in the heavens
and on the earth,
blood and fire and billows of smoke.
The sun will be turned to darkness
and the moon to blood
before the coming of the great and dreadful day of
the Lord.
And everyone who calls
on the name of the Lord will be saved;
for on Mount Zion and in Jerusalem
there will be deliverance,
as the Lord has said,
even among the survivors
whom the Lord calls."   Joel 2:28-32

God is exhaling His Spirit onto His people. It is an exciting time to be a part of a great harvest revival! I pray God will guide you exactly where He wants you and give you new assignments from Him.

We are living in a time and season where we need to pray in faith, and we need to walk in step with the Spirit. When we spend time in God's Presence and enter into His rest, He can do great things! I pray that you will have eyes to see and ears to hear the Lord as you seek Him and continue your journey to pray prophetically in line with His heart. Now is the time to walk in the Spirit!

Endnotes

Chapter 1 Bob Hazlett, visit www.bobhazlett.org
        "Now Is The Time" Podcast
Chapter 3: Heidi Baker, visit www.irisglobal.org
Chapter 4: Beth Moore, (2009) *Praying God's Word,* B&H
Books, visit www.lproof.org
Chapter 7: Sara Nicholls, "Purposeful Worship" Sermon,
        www.youtu.be/yP5XpM5MTzo
Chapter 8: Doug Addison, visit www.dougaddison.com
Chapter 10: Dennis Cramer, visit www.denniscramer.com
        Doug Addison, visit www.dougaddison.com
Chapter 12: Angie Smith, visit www.angiesmithonline.com
Chapter 16: Francis Frangipane, visit www.frangipane.org
Chapter 17: David Hogan, visit www.freedom-ministries.us
Chapter 18: Julie Meyer, visit www.juliemeyerministries.com

About the author:

Lori Granniss lives in Shelby, North Carolina. She is a prophetic intercessor, speaker, and writer. She writes on the blog, www.inspirehopemagazine.com . She loves to see God set people free. She is wife to David and mother to Landon and Logan.

www.ingramcontent.com/pod-product-compliance
Lightning Source LLC
Chambersburg PA
CBHW051838040426
42447CB00006B/586